Felt so Good

Over 30 irresistibly cute, cosy & colourful felted projects

Betz White

David and Charles

David & Charles is an F+W Publications Inc. company
4700 East Galbraith Road
Cincinnati, OH 45236

First published in the UK in 2008
First published in the USA in 2008 as *Warm Fuzzies* by
North Light Books, Cincinnati, Ohio

A catalogue record for this book is available from the
British Library.

ISBN-13: 978-0-7153-2847-7 paperback
ISBN-10: 0-7153-2847-6 paperback

Printed in China by SNP Leefung Printers Limited
for David & Charles
Brunel House   Newton Abbot   Devon

Visit our website at www.davidandcharles.co.uk

David & Charles books are available from all good
bookshops; alternatively you can contact our
Orderline on 0870 9908222 or write to us at FREEPOST EX2
110, D&C Direct, Newton Abbot, TQ12 4ZZ
(no stamp required UK only)

Editor: Jessica Gordon
Designer: Amanda Dalton
Production Coordinator: Greg Nock
Photographers: Tim Grondin, Christine Polomsky
Stylist: Nora Martini
Pattern Technician: Lisa Duwell

Special thanks to the helpful people at
Gorman Heritage Farm in Evendale, Ohio,
for providing a beautiful photography location,
and also for welcoming us so warmly.

Acknowledgments

It takes a village to write a book! Many
thanks to my editor, Jessica Gordon, and to
my agents, Lilly Ghahremani and Stefanie
Von Borstel, for navigating me through the
world of publishing. Also thanks to Tonia
Davenport, Amanda Dalton, Christine
Polomsky, Nora Martini, Tim Grondin and
everyone at F+W for believing in me.

Special thanks:

To my mom, for teaching me how
to sew and for always encouraging
my creativity.

To my dad, for his support and his
"weaselly" business expertise.

To my brothers and their wives, for being
constant sources of artistic influence.

To my Monday night knitting buddies,
for their encouragement.

To Grace Meacham, for pushing my
creativity and guiding my education.

To Sheryl Page, for seeing my strengths
and teaching me to swim with the sharks.

And to the wonderful residents
of Blogland, for connecting me to a
community of crafters worldwide.

Last but not least, thanks to my
wonderful husband and children. I couldn't
have done this without your continuous
support, multitudes of hugs and bottomless
cups of coffee.

About the Author

Betz White is known for her unique take on the art of felting—using castaway sweaters to create what she calls "felted wool, artfully stitched." Her designs reflect everyday objects in a fresh light, with a splash of wit and whimsy.

Betz's grandmother Frances was the first to notice her quirky style and flair for fashion. (Maybe it was the way three-year-old Betz colored the white toes of her saddle shoes with a red crayon. "They just needed something," she explained.) Betz's family always supported her creativity, providing her with a "crafty childhood" in the 1970s. Her mom taught her how to sew, knit and experiment with everything from papier mâché to macramé. Along with her brothers, Betz was encouraged to create things and develop her imagination, a practice she brought forward into adulthood.

Today a prolific felter, sewer and knitter, Betz sells her one-of-a-kind recycled wool items across the globe. Her work is regularly featured in a variety of magazines, Web sites and blogs. She teaches workshops, and she shares her felting tips and techniques on her blog at www.betzwhite.com. An artist with nearly two decades of professional design experience in the apparel industry, Betz is always challenging herself—and now her readers—with something fresh and new.

Betz lives in Maryland with her husband, Dave, her sons, Conner and Sean, and way, way too many felted sweaters.

Photograph by Chris Elinchev

Dedication

To the sweetest brown-eyed "boys" in my life, Dave, Conner and Sean. I love you.

contents

"Invention, my dear friends, is 93 percent perspiration, 6 percent electricity, 4 percent evaporation, and 2 percent butterscotch ripple."

Inspiration can strike us at the oddest times. And the most exhilarating feeling comes over us when it does. One of my favorite "Aha!" moments was the day I had the idea for my felted cupcake pincushions. That day I had taken a break from my work to read stories and snuggle with my youngest son. The next thing I knew, I was drifting off to the land of nod, surrounded by all the colorful scraps of ribbing left over from my many felted sweater projects. In my dream the ribbing took the form of the paper wrappers on cupcakes. That's it! Cupcakes! And so an idea was hatched.

Some people get great ideas in the shower or during their morning commute. I get mine when I'm drifting off to sleep or just waking up. (I've got a notebook on my nightstand just for that reason.) The point is, there is creativity in all of us waiting to be set free. The projects in *Warm Fuzzies* were designed to do just that—jump start your creativity by offering you tips, tools and techniques to make your own "dreams" come true.

Like my cupcake pincushions, all the projects in this book use a material I love working with—felted wool. During fashion design school, I was introduced to this medium. I learned about fibers and how felting knitted wool can transform it into a completely different fabric. I found it intriguing and liberating that I could knit, felt and then sew the resulting fabric into whatever I desired.

introduction

Eventually, it was my lack of patience that became a point of discovery. Instant gratification being what it is, I began to focus on felting wool that was already knit—secondhand sweaters! Felt first, then sew. That's my philosophy, and it's the method you'll find throughout *Warm Fuzzies*. I'll show you how to felt thrift-store sweaters, then cut them up and sew them into warm and whimsical projects for the whole family.

You'll find that using recycled materials is its own exercise in creativity. Taking an object out of context can teach us to see its underlying potential, adding a new dimension of beauty to whatever we create. For example, check out the *Just Right Tote* (page 118) to see how a striped sweater turns into a stylish bag. Or make your own *Cutie Pie Felt Bowls* (page 80) with two simple circles and a handful of felt balls. Sew up a pair of soft, warm mittens (page 114) with bits and pieces of cast-off sweaters in colors that will keep you happy during the cold, drab winter.

Take your pick of the colorful projects inside *Warm Fuzzies* and explore the versatility of felted wool. Wool is breathable and repels spills. Its elasticity allows for garments that are comfortable and hold their shape. And repurposing wool sweaters has an added advantage. I may be just a lazy knitter, but I like to think I am also honoring a commitment to living "green" by reusing old sweaters. You can feel good about using secondhand materials,

especially if you buy them from a charity-based thrift store.

As I developed the collection presented in this book, I focused on bringing fresh color combinations and elements of fun to the projects. Now it's up to you to express yourself through color choice and personal flair. I encourage you to seek out inspiration and to be in tune to it when it strikes. Take a break from routine. Slow down, smell the flowers, take a nap if necessary! It is the times when we are most relaxed and happy that the best ideas will come to us.

I am thrilled to be able to share my designs and my love of felting wool with you. I hope you will enjoy the time you spend making these projects, and I hope they will excite your imagination as much as they excite mine.

— Betz

Clockwise from left to right: a stack of felted sweaters, a jar of felt balls, felted I-cord, a stack of wool craft felt, wool yarn, more felt balls with straight pins.

deconstructing a sweater

To make the projects in the book, you'll need to learn a little about the main material you'll be working with: felted wool. What is felt? True felt is an unconstructed fabric made of wool fibers bonded together. In the presence of heat, moisture and friction, wool fibers shrink and bond together, resulting in a thick, dense material. For the projects in this book, we will be "felting" knitted wool from recycled sweaters. (This process is technically called *fulling*, though most people in the crafting world refer to it as *felting*.) The following guidelines tell you everything you'll need to know to get started.

Step One: Hunting and Gathering

You'll need to scour your closets and the local thrift shops for wool sweaters to felt. Get ready to read content and care labels. One hundred percent wool will typically give you the best results. However, other animal fibers, such as mohair or angora, will felt when combined with wool. Stay away from synthetics like acrylic and nylon, as they will not felt. (A little nylon is OK—but no more than 10 percent.) Check the care labels to make sure the wool is *not* washable. Usually the more strict the care label is (i.e., dry-clean only), the better the sweater will felt.

Step Two: Making the Transformation

Now that you've scored a few woolly finds, it's time for a little science experiment. Put up to five or six sweaters in the washer with regular laundry detergent along with a tennis ball or flip-flop. The detergent helps the fibers move against each other, and the tennis ball adds a little friction. Wash the sweaters on the hot water setting.

If you are felting only one or two sweaters at a time, keep the water level low. A high water level causes the sweaters to float on the top. With less friction they will be less likely to felt. Wash like colors together to prevent the transfer of one color fiber onto another.

After one cycle, check the sweaters for degree of felting. Shrinkage is challenging to predict due to different processes used in manufacturing. If you don't see much change or if the knit stitches are still visible, run it through another cycle. In my experience, top loaders with an agitator typically felt wool faster than front loaders.

After you have achieved your desired result, the felted sweaters can air dry or be put in the dryer on low for even more shrinkage. Remove when almost dry, not bone dry. Be sure to clean the lint traps well on both the washer and the dryer. If you felt load after load of sweaters, it's best to run a cycle of bleach through the washer to help remove any remaining fibers missed by the traps.

Step Three: Taking the Heat and Making the Cut

After felting a sweater, you may need to steam press the pieces flat. Always use the wool setting with steam on your iron. Dry heat will ruin your beautiful felt by making it crunchy! Press the felt from the wrong side or use a press cloth to cover your work.

Tips + Tricks for Felty Goodness

The Good, the Bad and the Ugly. *Felting is more of an art than a science. Some sweaters felt really easily. Usually, looser knits give the fibers a little room to grab on to each other and felt densely. Tighter knits with highly twisted yarns leave less room for friction and don't felt as much. Sometimes bad things happen to good sweaters, even when we follow all the "rules." If felting goes too far, the result can be stiff and boardy. Once felting occurs, there is no going back. Felting is forever! So take care to check your felting regularly. If you end up with a super-stiff material, try using it to make a project requiring some stability, like the Just Right Tote (see page 118) or the Mixed Messenger Bag (see page 108).*

Next Runner Up. *Let wool craft felt play a supporting role to your felted knits. It is a good weight for appliqués and backings. One hundred percent wool craft felt is beautiful but pricey. I prefer a nylon blend. To rid the felt of its hard, flat "manufactured" look, fill a sink with hot water and soak it for twenty minutes. Gently squeeze out the water and dry it in the dryer on medium until almost dry, not bone dry.*

Unsightly Ridges. *Often sweater sleeves will acquire a permanent ridge down the length of the sleeve during felting. To prevent this, cut the sleeves off the sweater before felting. Open up the underarm seam of the sleeve so the entire piece is flat rather than tube-like. This will allow it to felt more evenly.*

Ditch the Itch. *The softer the sweater is before felting, the softer it will be afterward. Keep this in mind, especially for wearable projects. If you have sensitive skin, try using a wool/cashmere blend.*

Depending on the project, sometimes it's handy to take advantage of features your felted sweater already has. Leave the ribbing, necklines, pockets, etc. intact and use them as details in the final project. On the flip side, keep in mind that any moth holes you started with will not close up during felting. These can easily be cut around or covered by an appliqué.

Don't be afraid to dive right in and start cutting! One of the best features of felted wool is that it won't unravel. You'll need sharp scissors to cut your felt. A rotary cutter, mat and straightedge are also great tools when measuring and cutting large rectangles.

Clockwise from bottom left: sewing thread, embroidery floss, chalk liner, seam ripper, pincushions, felted sweater scraps, measuring tape, fabric glue, rotary cutter on top of clear straightedge.

gathering materials

I sewed all the projects in the book with a sewing machine, although some of the smaller ones could certainly be sewn by hand. To get the same look as the projects shown, you'll need a sewing machine that can do basic straight and zigzag stitches. Sewing with felt is a linty business, so keep your machine clean and lubricated for best results. All the patterns (beginning on page 127) include seam allowances. Simply enlarge the pattern on a copier as indicated and cut it out. Grain line, an arrow showing alignment of pattern to fabric, will be indicated if it is pertinent to the project.

General Supplies

In addition to a sewing machine, you should gather a few general sewing supplies and some crafting supplies to create the projects in this book. If you're a crafter and/or a sewer, you probably already have most of these simple tools and materials.

Needles: You'll need a selection of needles for the different kinds of hand sewing you'll do for these projects. Use all-purpose sewing needles to seam up the gaps left by stuffing or to hand sew small projects. Use embroidery needles with larger eyes to accommodate several strands of embroidery floss when you add embellished features and decorative embroidered stitches. Keep a tapestry needle with a large eye on hand to add embellishments with thicker yarn.

Pins: Heavy-duty straight pins are indispensable for any sewing project. Use pins liberally to keep your seams straight, and keep a pincushion or a magnetic pin keeper handy to receive your pins once they've finished their jobs.

Thread: You'll always need all-purpose thread for machine and hand sewing, so keep spools on hand to match the fabrics you'll be sewing with. And don't forget to wind plenty of bobbins in the same colors.

Embroidery Floss: This multistranded, colorful thread is used to add decorative embroidered stitches. Generally speaking, you'll want to separate the thread into two- or three-ply strands instead of using it all together.

Yarn: Wool yarn looks great with felted wool—keep a selection in different colors around. You don't need much. If you're a knitter, this is a great way to put your scraps to good use.

Fabric Glue: No, this isn't cheating. It's simplification. Use all-purpose or washable fabric glue for garments.

Fusible Webbing: This stuff is great. Stock up on medium-weight, double-sided sheets of fusible webbing, and you'll be ready to go to town on your appliqués.

Seam Ripper: Even the best of us make mistakes, and a seam ripper makes taking out stitches at least a little less painful.

Scissors: Use a separate pair for paper and dedicate your sharpest shears for use on fabric only. Embroidery sharps come in handy for detailed cuts and for trimming threads.

Rotary Cutter, Mat and Straightedge: The combination of a rotary cutter, a rubber mat with marked measurements and a handy straightedge for neat cuts is optional, but the trio works great for cutting straight pieces.

Disappearing Marker or Chalk Liner: These tools are indispensable for making temporary marks on fabric. A marking pen works best on smooth, light-colored fabrics. Use a chalk liner for darker, fuzzier fabrics.

Needle-Felting Tools

Needle felting is a fun and easy way to add design elements to solid felt. Here's how it works: Special felting needles with barbs at their tips create friction between wool fabric and wool roving or yarn, causing the two materials to become felted together. Always clean your needles with alcohol before starting and wear eye protection, just in case! These needles are sharp, so be careful.

Felting needles are very sharp needles with tiny barbs on them that cause friction when poked though material. They come in various sizes, or gauges. For basic techniques, use a medium size/gauge.

Wool roving is an untwisted "rope" of parallel wool fibers. Roving can be used for all forms of felting as well as for spinning into yarn.

Use a **block of foam** under your work to "needle" into. Any standard foam used for cushions is suitable.

The **Clover needle-felting tool** holds multiple needles and is designed to be used with the Clover **brush mat**.

From top to bottom, left to right: (top row) wool roving, (middle row) needle-felting tool and brush mat, (bottom row) wool yarn.

techniques to learn

Master the basic skills in this section, and you'll be able to easily make all of the projects inside *Warm Fuzzies*.

Sewing
Sewing with felted knits is a real treat. The material is so forgiving. It can be cut without fraying and shaped by steaming. Raw edges can be zigzagged together or straight stitched with minimal seam allowances. Plus, seams require no finishing...woo-hoo!

Seaming Techniques
There are several machine seaming techniques used throughout the projects in the book. Each one can help you achieve a different look.

Straight Stitch Seam
Pin fabric with right sides together. Leave a ⅛" to ¼" (3mm to 6mm) seam allowance and use a stitch length of 3.5 to 4. Press seam allowances open from the wrong side. Snip and notch curves before turning right-side out.

Zigzag Stitch Seam
This seam is ideal for patching together smaller pieces of felt because the join creates a smooth front and back with no seam allowances. It is the least bulky seaming technique, and it's also great for sewing curves. Butt together cut edges, right-sides up. Zigzag stitch with a width of 4 and a stitch length of 2.5. Press from the wrong side.

Lapped Seam
With right-sides up, place one edge over another, overlapping by ½" (1cm). Pin and straight stitch down the center of the overlap, leaving a ¼" (6mm) seam allowance on each side.

Embroidery Stitches
Embroidery is a pretty way to add a little embellishment. If you're using embroidery floss, separate it into three-ply strands and thread it onto an embroidery needle. Pair a fingering weight yarn with a tapestry needle.

French Knot
French knots can be the perfect touch where your embroidery just needs a tiny something: the eye of a bird, the dot on a ladybug. If you've never tried it before, practice first on a scrap until you perfect your technique.

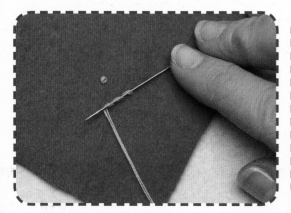 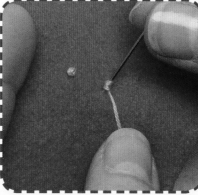

1. Wrap thread
Bring the needle up through the fabric at the desired position. Working close to the fabric, wrap the thread around the needle three times.

2. Create knot
Holding on to the thread with your left hand, insert the point of the needle into the fabric close to where the thread first emerged. Keeping the thread wraps close to the fabric and holding the thread taut, pull the needle and thread through to the back. Secure on the back for a single French knot or bring the needle through to the front at the position of the next knot.

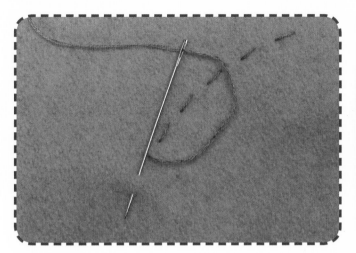

Running Stitch

Pass the needle over and under the fabric, making the stitches on the surface of equal length. The stitches on the back side should also be of equal length, but shorter than the upper stitches.

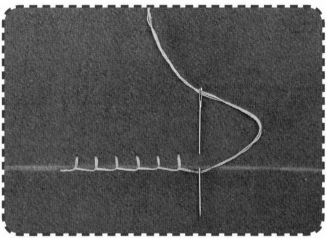

Blanket Stitch

Start with the thread coming up through the fabric from the line. Insert the needle above the line, taking a straight downward stitch and emerging on the line. As the needle is pulled through, the thread stays under the needle point. Pull the stitch to form a loop and repeat. This stitch may also be used along an edge.

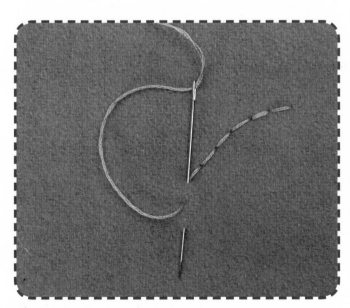

Backstitch

Bring the thread up through the fabric on the stitch line, and then take a small backward stitch through the fabric. Bring the needle through again a little in front of the first stitch. Take another stitch backward, inserting the needle at the point where it first came through.

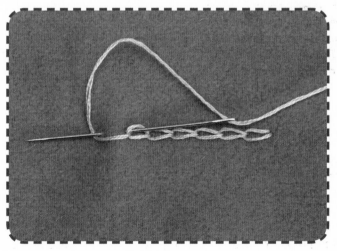

Chain Stitch

Bring the thread up through the fabric on the stitch line and hold it down with your left thumb. Insert the needle where it last emerged and bring the point up through the fabric a short distance away. Pull the thread through, keeping the working thread under the needle point. Repeat.

Fusing

Fusible webbing is an excellent tool for appliqué. There are several types on the market to choose from. I suggest using a standard weight that has a paper backing on at least one side.

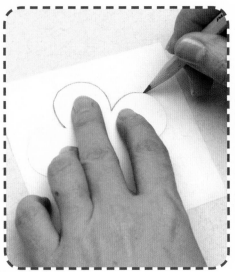

1. Trace image onto fusible web

Using a pencil, trace around a pattern piece onto the paper side of the webbing. (Remember to reverse the image if necessary, as this will end up as the back of the appliqué.)

2. Peel backing away from web

If your webbing has paper on both sides, peel away the plain paper backing. If not, just place the image, web-side down, onto the back of the felt you wish to fuse.

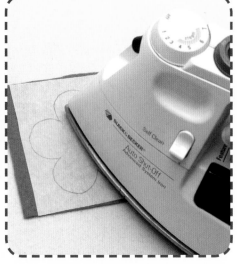

3. Iron web onto felt to fuse

Following the manufacturer's directions, fuse the webbing by ironing on the paper side with the image. (This usually requires a hot, dry iron.)

4. Cut out shape

Using sharp scissors, trim away excess felt, following the traced outline of the image.

5. Peel off backing and fuse to fabric

Remove remaining paper from the felt shape. Place it web-side down onto the fabric to which you wish to fuse the shape.

6. Stitch, embroider or cut out element

If the image is being used as an appliqué, stitch it into place, add embroidered detail, or leave as is. See the following page for more information on appliqué. If you'd like to use the image as a two-sided motif, as in an ornament or brooch, trim out the element, following the edge with scissors.

Appliqué

Appliqué is an embellishment term for cutting pieces of one fabric and applying them to the surface of another. There are several machine- and hand-applied versions of this technique.

Traditional

The most common type of appliqué is the traditional machine-sewn technique.

Set the machine on zigzag with a stitch width of 4 and a length of 2.5. After fusing the appliqué motif into position, carefully zigzag stitch around the motif so the stitches cover the edge of the shape, securing it to the background fabric. For a crisper edge, straight stitch (2.5L) around the edge of the appliqué as shown above.

Tacking

This technique creates a casual feeling and adds dimension to the project.

Cut out a motif from the desired fabric. Do not use fusible webbing. Simply hand-tack the shape into place with matching or contrasting thread or yarn.

Reverse Appliqué

This type of appliqué is useful for any project where both sides will be visible, such as a blanket.

1. Stitch appliqué in place

Pin the appliqué motif into position onto the background fabric. (Do not fuse it with webbing.) Straight stitch around the motif, ⅛" (3mm) in from the edge.

2. Trim away background fabric

Turn the work over. Insert the sharp tip of embroidery scissors into the back of the piece and carefully trim away the background fabric behind the stitched motif, about ⅛" (3mm) inside the stitch line.

Needle Felting

Needle felting is a fast no-sew way to add decorative details to your project. Felting needles have tiny barbs on them that cause friction when poked through fiber and fabric. As you punch the fibers with the needle in a repetitive up-and-down motion, you will see the materials begin to felt together.

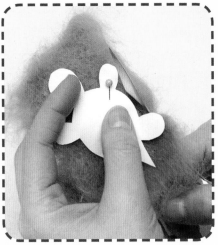

1. Needle felt roving

Lay out two thin cross-hatched layers of roving on top of the needle-felting brush. Punch the layered fibers repeatedly with the needle tool on the mat (or with a single needle on a foam block) until the fibers felt together. Carefully remove the fused fibers from the brush or mat.

2. Cut out shape from felted roving

Cut out a paper pattern and pin it to the felted fiber. Cut around the motif.

3. Needle felt shape to wool piece

Place the motif onto the background fabric on top of the felting brush or foam block. Starting in the center, needle felt the motif into place, punching with the tool until the motif has completely felted to the fabric.

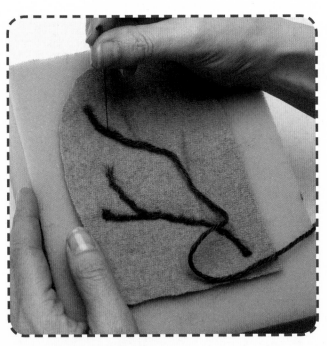

4. Needle felt embellishment from roving

For a more free-form result, lay down a length of roving onto the work you wish to embellish. Twist the end of the roving between your fingers and needle the end into place. Continue to gently twist and lay down the roving as you go.

Use a single needle to needle felt a piece of wool yarn

For a precise outline, needle felt a single strand of wool yarn along a premarked line, or along the edge of an appliqué. Use low-twist yarn for best results. Use a single needle only when felting on top of a foam mat.

I-Cord

There are several ways to make I-cord. It can be knit on double-pointed knitting needles or with the use of a "knitting spool." There are many variations to the knitting spool, the fastest of which is the crank-operated spool.

Creating Felted I-Cord

To make felted I-cord, use a fingering-weight wool yarn. After making the I-cord, place it in a lingerie bag and wash it in the washing machine with hot water. You can put it in the same load with sweaters you are felting if the colors are similar. Expect the length to shrink by about 25 percent, depending on the type of yarn used.

Using Your Felted I-Cord

Felted I-cord can be used in many ways to trim and embellish felted projects. As with other felted knits, it can be cut without unraveling. It adds dimension and is an easy way to make a clean finished edge.

Sewing on I-Cord as Border

Using the widest zigzag stitch, butt the cut edge of a piece of sweater felt against a length of I-cord. Stitch slowly without stretching, allowing the zigzag stitching to straddle both the felt and the I-cord. After stitching, steam press from the wrong side to flatten any rippling that may have occurred.

Doubling I-Cord

Follow the directions as for sewing on an I-cord edge, only butt together two pieces of I-cord. Zigzag stitch down the center of the two I-cords without stretching them. This will create a wider trim piece suitable for a strap, handle or border.

Whipstitching I-Cord in Place

Place a length of I-cord along a seam or edge. Handstitch with matching or contrasting yarn by bringing the needle up through the fabric on one side of the I-cord, crossing over the I-cord perpendicularly, then stitching back down into the fabric on the other side.

the felted nest

Your home is your nest. It's where you find shelter to be yourself and seek comfort in the things that define you.

This chapter guides you in making six decorative and functional projects for the home. I created these designs to provide a starting point. Your choice of recycled materials allows you to customize each design to reflect your personal style. Soft and dense as well as warm and fuzzy, felted wool is the perfect companion for cozying up and hunkering down.

Whether it's the casual *Rustic Throw* (page 20) or the cheeky *Breakfast-in-Bed Pillow* (page 30), you're bound to find the perfect accent to express the personality of your home.

rustic throw

Snuggle up with the *Rustic Throw*, and give a warm and personal touch to your living room decor. Easy lapped seams create a casual look. Reverse appliqué lends added dimension and an element of whimsy.

Hit the bargain day at your local thrift store and come home with an armful of colorful sweaters. Find an incredible stripe? Let it be your inspiration. One sweater can set the color palette for your project. Look for solid colors that coordinate and accent the stripe.

Sweaters of similar weight are most compatible. Large rectangles from five or six sweaters patch together to make this clean and simple design.

materials

5 to 6 large felted sweaters in compatible colors

accent yarn

sewing machine

scissors

ruler or straightedge

tapestry needle

straight pins

rotary cutter and mat (optional)

masking tape

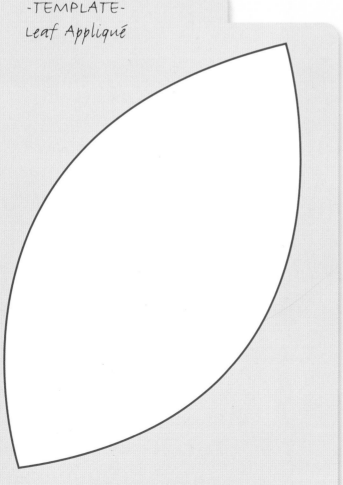

-TEMPLATE-
Leaf Appliqué

Template for leaf appliqué shown here at actual size.

Planning Your Throw

When planning your throw, decide on a general finished dimension. The project shown is about 45" x 60" (114cm x 152cm), fitting for the back of a couch and a nice size for snuggling. When cutting the large rectangles, I prefer to use a rotary cutter, metal straightedge and mat, but large scissors will work as well. Minimize waste as you cut, making the rectangles as large as possible. Lay them out on the floor to plan the placement of pattern, color and appliqué. Trim as needed to create three to four columns of equal length. Before sewing, I like to number each one using a bit of masking tape to help me remember the placement of each piece.

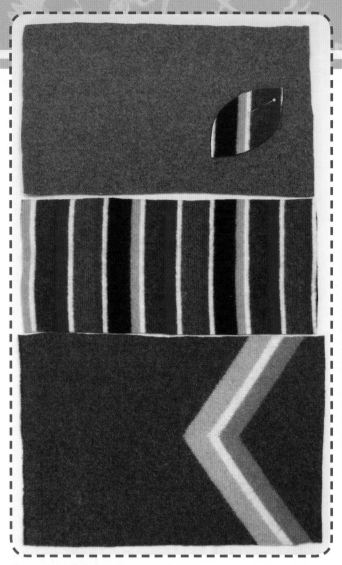

1. Cut out and arrange first column

Cut the felted sweaters into large rectangles of the same width, but of varying lengths. Use a variety of the scraps to cut leaf appliqué shapes (see template, page 21). Place each leaf appliqué on the desired rectangle and pin into place. Repeat to create two to three more columns, depending on the size you'd like your blanket to be. (My columns are about 15" [38cm] wide by 60" [152cm] long.)

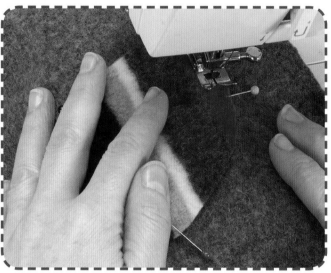

2. Sew on reverse appliqué leaves

Straight stitch around each leaf shape with a sewing machine. Set your machine to a large stitch length (4), working ¼" (6mm) in from the raw edge of the leaf.

3. Cut away back of leaf

Turn the work over. Using small sharp-tipped scissors, trim away the background fabric ¼" (6mm) inside the stitch line, so the leaf shape is visible from the back of the blanket as well as from the front.

4. Add decorative stitching to leaves

Working from the front side of the blanket, use accent yarn to handstitch a "vein" up the center of the leaf. Repeat steps 2 through 4 for all leaves.

5. Sew rectangles into column

Starting with the first column, overlap the edge of the top rectangle over the second rectangle by ½" (1cm). Pin across overlap. Straight stitch with the sewing machine down the center of the overlap, creating a ¼" (6mm) seam allowance on the front and back of the work. Repeat down the entire column, creating a "shingle" effect. Sew the remaining three columns, alternating the direction of overlap (first column down, next one up, etc.). See Techniques to Learn, page 12, for further instructions on sewing a lapped seam.

6. Sew columns together

Once the columns are sewn together, assemble them following the same "shingle" technique across the work.

7. Sew ribbed strips together

Zigzag stitch strips of ribbing together so they are as long as one of the short sides of the blanket. Make a second ribbing strip to border the remaining short side of the blanket.

8. Sew ribbing border to blanket

Straight stitch the ribbing border to each short end of the blanket.

9. Add decorative stitching

Use a tapestry needle and fingering-weight or sport-weight yarn to add decorative stitching along the ribbed borders of the blanket.

nest family album

materials

9" x 9" (23cm x 23cm)
(or any size) photo album

felted sweaters,
striped and solid

9" x 21" (23cm x 53cm)
rectangle of wool craft felt

wool craft felt scraps
in various colors

double-sided fusible web

approx 2½ yds (2m)
felted I-cord

buttons

yarn

embroidery floss in color
scheme similar to sweaters

sewing machine

iron and press cloth

scissors

ruler

pencil

chalk liner

needle

straight pins

Whether your family tree is in full foliage or just sprouting, everyone needs a family album. This album is a cozy place to tuck your memories.

This project is easily customized to fit any size photo album or scrapbook. Start by selecting a sturdy hardcover album. Choose some well-loved sweaters to full for the felted and stitched cover. Embellish with a charming bird appliqué, adding personalized details as you wish.

This artfully stitched album is great as a gift to a new mom, a happy housewarming offering or a lovely addition to your own little nest.

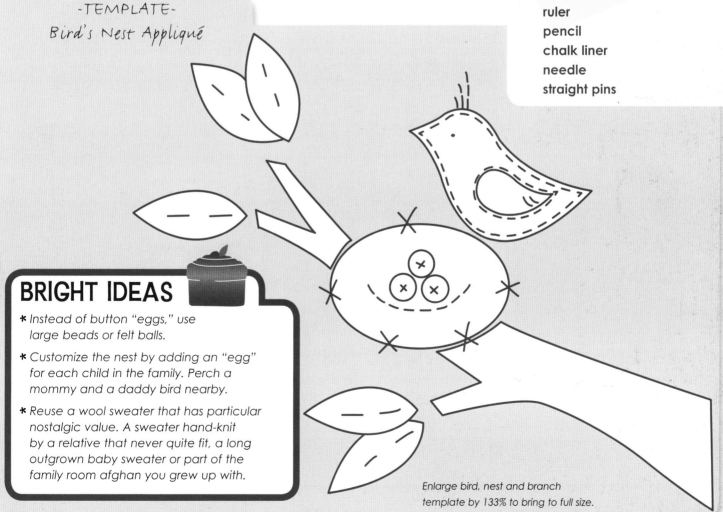

-TEMPLATE-
Bird's Nest Appliqué

BRIGHT IDEAS

* Instead of button "eggs," use large beads or felt balls.

* Customize the nest by adding an "egg" for each child in the family. Perch a mommy and a daddy bird nearby.

* Reuse a wool sweater that has particular nostalgic value. A sweater hand-knit by a relative that never quite fit, a long outgrown baby sweater or part of the family room afghan you grew up with.

Enlarge bird, nest and branch
template by 133% to bring to full size.

1. Cut fabric for outside and lining

Open the photo album and measure the total area of the inside of the book from cover to cover. Cut a piece of craft felt to those dimensions. For the album shown, the dimensions are 9" x 21" (23cm x 53cm). Measure the front cover of the album and the spine. Cut pieces of felt for the covers (9" x 9" [23cm x 23cm] as shown) and for the spine (9" x 3" [23cm x 8cm] as shown). Use craft felt for the lining and felted sweaters for the spine and front and back covers. Also collect several small felt scraps to use for the appliqué on the album cover.

2. Cut and pin cover pieces

Cut the squares for the covers along a curved line, following the pattern on page 127. Match up one half of the solid square with one half of the striped square. Place pins in each half of each square, lining them up along the curved edge. Butt together the edges of the curves, and use the pins as guides as you zigzag stitch the pieces together using a stitch length of 2.5 long and 4 wide. (See Techniques to Learn, page 12, for a close-up of a finished zigzag seam.)

3. Sew pieces together

Pin the spine panel to one side of the front panel with right sides together. Straight stitch the pieces together, leaving a ¼" (6mm) seam allowance. (See Techniques to Learn, page 12, for further instruction on sewing a straight seam.) Press the allowances open. Repeat to stitch the other side of the spine to the back panel.

4. Iron fusible web onto felt

Copy the templates on page 25, and trace each one onto the paper side of a sheet of fusible web in reverse. Fuse each one onto a piece of felt with an iron. (See Fusing, page 14, for more information.)

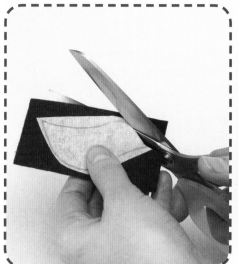

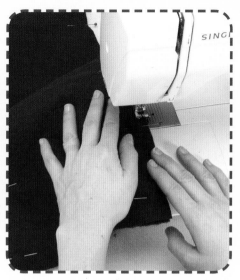

5. Cut out felt shapes

Cut along the pencil lines on the fusible web to cut out the felt shapes. Peel off the paper backing.

6. Sew around fused shapes on album cover

Arrange all the felt shapes onto the album cover to create a small scene. Finalize the placement of the pieces, then lay a press cloth over the entire arrangement and iron over the cloth to fuse the shapes to the cover. (See Techniques to Learn, pages 14–15, for step-by-step instructions on fusing and appliqué.) Stitch button "eggs" onto the nest with thread. Add decorative stitching with embroidery floss and yarn.

7. Sew lining to cover

Pin the finished cover to the lining with wrong sides together. Edge stitch the pieces together ⅛" (3mm) from the edge, lining-side up. Round the corners as you approach them. Press and trim the corners and other uneven edges of the sweater felt.

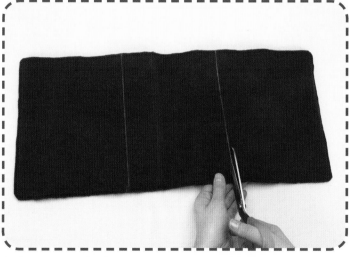

8. Cut slits in lining

With the lining facing up, mark two vertical lines with the chalk liner 7½" (19cm) in from each side edge. (Measurement varies depending on size of album.) With the tips of sharp scissors, snip a tiny opening at the bottom of each line. Take care not to cut through all the layers. Insert the scissors into the slit and cut along the line to the top edge. Repeat for the other line.

9. Finish cover with I-cord edging

For the I-cord edging, butt the I-cord against the panel edge and attach it with zigzag stitch around the perimeter of the cover. (See Techniques to Learn, page 17, for more information on sewing I-cord.) Hand stitch the I-cord ends together. (This step can be eliminated if desired.) Open the album, and insert the album cover into the slits in the lining.

scrapwork pillow

This is one of my favorite ways to use up scraps leftover from other felting projects. Whether you use a tonal collection of remnants or a crazy mixed-up kaleidoscope of colors, this pillow will add a splash of panache to any setting.

Similarly sized pieces are zigzagged together to form a continuous pillow top. A variety of patterns and textures create a mosaic of detail and interest. The pillow back can be solid or pieced as well. Casually tacked flower appliqués provide a playful accent, and felted I-cord trims the edge.

materials

16" x 16" (41cm x 41cm) pillow form

felted sweater scraps and 1 large piece for back

approx 2 yds (2m) felted I-cord

fingering-weight or sport-weight yarn

sewing machine

iron and press cloth

scissors

tapestry needle

sewing needle and thread

straight pins

1. Sew scraps into strips

Zigzag stitch (4W, 2.5L) sweater scraps together into strips at least 16" (41cm) long and of varying widths, depending on the size of the scraps you're using. Sew enough strips to make a 16" x 16" (41cm x 41cm) square. See Techniques to Learn, page 12, for a close-up of zigzag stitch.

2. Sew strips together into square

Sew the strips together with a zigzag stitch to make a 16" x 16" (41cm x 41cm) square. The edges of the square may be irregular. You'll trim them down to size later. Steam press the square flat from the wrong side.

3. Sew flowers onto pillow front

Use the templates on page 127 to cut out flowers and centers of flowers from two colors of felt scraps. Layer the flower centers on top of the flowers and use yarn threaded on a tapestry needle to cross-stitch through the layers, securing the flower to the front of the pillow. Repeat for the remaining flowers.

4. Trim irregular edges

Cut out a 16" (41cm) square of felted sweater in a solid color for the back of the pillow. Lay the front and back of the pillow on your work surface with right sides together and the back of the pillow on top. Trim away the irregular edges of the front of the pillow, using the back of the pillow as a guide.

With right sides facing, straight stitch the front and back of the pillow together, leaving a ¼" (6mm) seam allowance. Leave a 6" (15cm) gap at the top of the pillow cover to insert the pillow form. Trim seam allowances at the corners. Insert the pillow form and baste the opening closed with needle and thread.

5. Whipstitch on I-cord border

Pin the felted I-cord into the sewn seam of the pillow. Using fingering- or sport-weight yarn, sew the I-cord to the edge of the pillow with a whipstitch spaced about ¼" (6mm) apart. See Techniques to Learn, page 17, for more detailed instructions on whipstitching I-cord into place.

tip For extra stability, glue the I-cord onto the pillow edge wtih fabric glue before stitching.

breakfast-in-bed pillow

Breakfast in bed on a weekday? C'mon, you deserve it. Served up warm and felty with a side of silly, this pillow is sure to start your day off with a smile.

This design was inspired by the expression, "Wakey, wakey, eggs and bakey!" Create felted I-cord to accent plates, make toast crust and even to create a flower stem. To enhance the dimensional feel, each item on the menu is made to order, then tacked in place.

Part of a complete breakfast, this work of art would be a great addition to a guest room. Better yet, keep it on your own bed and make every morning feel like the weekend.

materials

16" x 16" (41cm x 41cm) pillow form

felted sweaters

wool craft felt

approx. 13' (4m) felted I-cord in various colors

double-sided fusible web

fiberfill

embroidery floss

beads for strawberry

fabric glue

sewing machine

straight pins

needle and thread

iron and press cloth

scissors

pencil

marking pen

Before beginning this project, make the plate, napkin and grapefruit bowl according to the following measurements:

Center plate:
circle 6½" (17cm) in diameter
Plate rim: circle 9" (23cm) in diameter
Napkin: 8" x 3¾"
(20cm x 10cm) rectangle
Bowl: circle 4½" (11cm) in diameter

Cut the front and back of an extra-large felted sweater into two 16" x 16" (41cm x 41cm) squares. Use one as the front of the pillow, and set the other square aside for the back of the pillow. Using the patterns (see pages 128–129) and the dimensions provided, cut out all the elements using felted sweater scraps. Piece together with zigzag seaming, if needed for larger pieces (such as the plate or the large pillow squares). Make and felt I-cord in desired colors.

Preparing Your Pillow Project

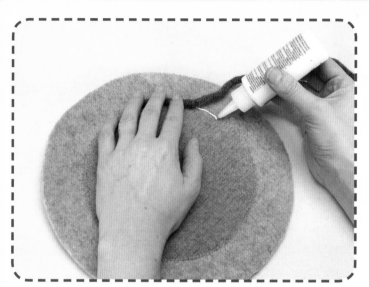

1. Create plate

Zigzag stitch the rim of the plate to the the center circle. Glue the blue I-cord onto the plate with fabric glue, concealing the seam. Pin the I-cord in place until the glue dries.

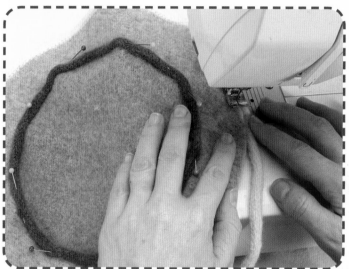

2. Sew cream I-cord onto outer rim of plate

Zigzag stitch the cream I-cord around the outer rim of the plate. Zigzag stitch the cream I-cord around the grapefruit bowl. Handstitch the ends of the I-cord together with matching thread for the plate and the bowl.

3. Sew main elements onto pillow

Use the template on page 128 to trace the fork onto the paper side of a sheet of fusible web. Then fuse the fork to gray craft felt and cut it out. Fuse the fork to a colorful "napkin." Hand embroider around the edge with running stitch, if desired. Pin the plate, the grapefruit bowl and the napkin to the pillow where you'd like them to go. Sew all the elements into place. Sew the large plate along the inner I-cord onto the front cover of the pillow with a zipper foot. Zigzag stitch the napkin in place.

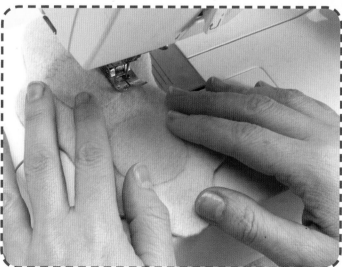

4. Make eggs

Cut out the egg shapes and two circles for yolks using the template on page 128. Fuse yolks to whites, zigzag stitching around edges.

31

5. Make grapefruit

Trace the section pattern onto the paper side of the fusible web. Fuse it to cream-colored felt. Cut out the "spokes" of the grapefruit. Fuse the spokes of the grapefruit to the felt grapefruit circle. Straight stitch along each of the spokes. Add an orange starburst at the center of the grapefruit with embroidery floss, if desired. Zigzag stitch the gold I-cord to the outside edge.

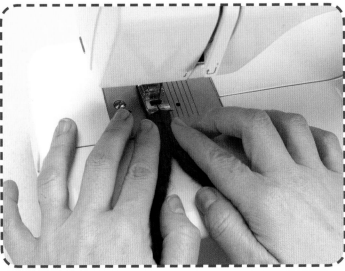

6. Make crust for toast

Fuse two layers of sweater felt together to make the toast. Use the template on page 128 to cut the fused felt into a toast shape. For the crust, zigzag stitch two lengths of brown felted I-cord together, equaling 20" (51cm) total (or the length of the perimeter of the toast).

7. Glue on I-cord crust

Apply fabric glue to the edge of the toast and press the I-cord crust into the glue. Pin the I-cord in place until it dries. Cut a butter pat out of yellow felt and glue it in the center of the toast.

8. Sew and stuff strawberry

Follow the templates on page 128 to cut out the strawberry and the strawberry top. Fold the strawberry piece in half with right sides together, and hand or machine stitch the side seam. Stuff the berry with a bit of fiberfill. Work in running stitch at the top edge of the berry, gather the fabric by pulling on the thread, and tie it off. If desired, hand stitch seed beads onto the strawberry with a beading needle.

9. Glue top on strawberry

Glue the leaf to the top of the strawberry, covering the gathered felt.

10. Make bacon

Refer to the templates on page 129 to cut a striped sweater long-ways into strips that look like bacon. Zigzag stitch brown I-cord to both edges of each bacon strip.

11. Snip felt for flower petals

Cut a piece of cream felt and a piece of pink felt into 2½" x 3" (6cm x 8cm) rectangles. Fold each felt piece in half lengthwise, and straight stitch the raw edges together. Snip the folded edges at ¼" (6mm) increments to create loops.

12. Stitch flower

Starting with the cream rectangle, roll the rectangle, hand-tacking the raw edge while rolling. Wrap the cream roll with the pink and tack them together.

BRIGHT IDEA

Would you prefer bagels and lox? Maybe you'd like to pay homage to Dr. Seuss with some green eggs and ham. Let your imagination (and your appetite) lead you to your own creative combination.

13. Tack all breakfast items to pillow

Pin all the food into place, using the plate, bowl and napkin as guides. Hand-tack the grapefruit into the bowl to secure it, following the gold I-cord edge. Hand-tack the toast, eggs and strawberry to the plate. Pin the bacon to the plate, allowing it to wave and curl, and hand-tack it in place. Tack the flower to the pillow above the plate, then use a marking pen to mark the placement of the I-cord stem and leaves. Tack the stem into place. With right sides facing, sew the front and back of the pillow together, leaving one side open. Take care not to catch the tacked-on elements in the seams. Turn right-side out, insert the pillow form, and then hand-stitch the pillow closed.

BRIGHT IDEA

To personalize your stocking even more, try needle felting a monogram on the cuff. (See Needle Felting in the Techniques to Learn section on page 16.) For example, add a simple initial, family position (dad or sister) or even nicknames, depending on how embarrassing they are!

christmas stockings

Handmade Christmas stockings are a long-time tradition in my family. This felted version is a twist on a classic. Clean and simple, crazy patchwork, sweetly embellished...the variations are endless. Here's your chance to mix it up and make one to suit every personality in your gang. Once you get started, you'll see how addicting this project is.

This pattern is easily scaled to any size you want. Bigger is better when it comes to stockings! Use one large sweater (cut the main stocking shape out of the front and back of a large sweater) or combine a few (create a patchwork by butting scraps together and zigzag stitching to create larger pieces). If you're making a collction for your family, consider repeating one design element (i.e., using a patch from the same sweater) in each variation to give the group a cohesive feel.

materials

- multiple felted sweaters
- yarn
- trims: felted I-cord, wool strips, buttons, felt balls
- large safety pin or tapestry needle for wool strip
- seam ripper (optional)
- sewing machine
- iron and press cloth
- scissors
- sleeve roll (optional)
- straight pins
- needle and thread
- fabric glue

1. Prepare stocking pieces

Using the patterns provided on pages 129–130, cut out two sets of pieces for the stocking, one set cut out in reverse for the back of the stocking. Lay out all the pieces for your stocking on your work surface, along with the materials you'll use for decorative trim.

2. Begin to seam stocking pieces together

Pin the toe piece of the stocking to the foot piece and seam them together with a straight stitch on the sewing machine, leaving a ¼" (6mm) seam allowance. (See Techniques to Learn, page 12, for further instruction on straight stitch seaming.) Repeat for the remaining pieces of the stocking for both front and back (except for the cuff). Press open all the seam allowances from the wrong side as you work. With right sides together, sew the front and back of the stocking together.

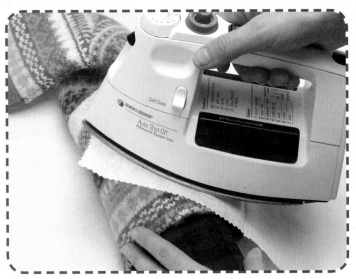

3. Steam stocking seams

Turn the stocking right-side out. Slide the sleeve roll into the stocking and cover the stocking with a press cloth. Steam press the stocking. (If you don't have a sleeve roll, you could roll up a small towel to place inside the stocking while pressing.)

4. Pin cuff and stocking hanger in place

Straight stitch the sides of the cuff with right sides together. Turn the cuff right-side out. Place the cuff inside the stocking, lining up the raw edges. (The right side of the cuff should be facing the wrong side of the stocking.) Place a 7" (18cm) loop of I-cord or another type of trim in between the cuff and stocking layers at the back of the stocking. Pin the loop into place, sandwiching it between the cuff and stocking. Straight stitch the pieces together with a sewing machine. Flip the cuff to the outside of the stocking and press it with a press cloth.

5. Thread wool strip through cuff

Thread a length of ¼"- (6mm) wide wool felt or other trim onto a safety pin or a large tapestry needle. Cut small slits at regular intervals in the ribs of the stocking cuff with a seam ripper, and lace the wool strip in and out of the rib cuff as an accent.

6. Add felted balls to ends of ties

Tie the wool strip into a bow and thread a felt ball onto the end of each tie. Try piercing the felt ball with an awl or small utility knife before threading it onto the end of the tie. Knot the end of each tie to secure the balls.

7. Add decorative stitching

Using a double strand of yarn, make cross-stitches around the heel and toe seams, if desired.

These simple flower shapes can spruce up a simple solid-color stocking. A felted yo-yo flower, a rosette or a simple daisy and button (see Scrapwork Pillow, page 28) can add an offbeat vibe to a traditional shape.

Yo-Yo Flower

1. Stitch around circle with running stitch

Cut out a circle of felt and work around the edge in loose running stitch. See Techniques to Learn, page 13, for a close-up of running stitch.

2. Pull circle into a "yo-yo"

Pull on the thread and cinch the circle into a flower shape. The edge of the circle will come into the middle of the flower.

3. Add flower center

Secure the center of the flower with a few stitches and tie off the thread. Glue a felt ball to the center of the flower with fabric glue.

Rosette

  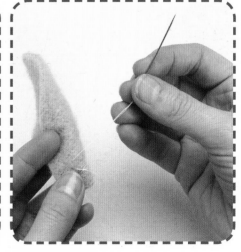

1. Work running stitch along edge

Use the template on page 129 to cut out a rosette shape from a felted sweater scrap. Work a loose running stitch along one edge of the strip.

2. Gather and roll

Gather the running stitch while rolling the rectangle into a rosette. Tack the gathered edge close to secure the flower.

3. Create leaf

Use the template on page 129 to cut out a leaf. Fold the leaf lengthwise and hand stitch a tuck from the wrong side. Tack the leaf to the base of the rosette.

christmas ornaments

Nothing says Christmas like a tree brimming with beautiful ornaments. Store bought or handmade, glass or fabric, side by side each ornament tells its own story. Adding a few new ones every year builds a wonderful collection for holidays to come.

Whip up a few of these for small gifts to keep on hand during the holidays. They also make for beautiful present toppers tied on with a bow.

Sweet Pear Ornament

1. Needle felt roving onto pear
Cut two pears out of yellow felted sweater scraps and two leaves out of green felted sweater scraps (see templates, page 131). Needle felt a wisp of yellow and then green roving onto the pear shapes to create shading. Remove the pear from the mat and steam press the needle-felted pear, covering it with a press cloth. See Techniques to Learn, page 16, for more information on needle felting.

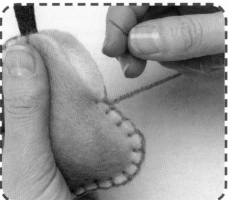

2. Blanket stitch pieces together and stuff pear
Fold a felt strip in half and pin it to the wrong side of one pear shape to create the stem hanger. With wrong sides together, blanket stitch the pear pieces together with green yarn. (See Techniques to Learn, page 13, for more detailed information on blanket stitch.) Start at the top, securing the stem first. Leave a 1" (3cm) opening, and stuff it with fiberfill. Continue with blanket stitch to close the pear.

3. Attach leaves
Sandwich the top of the pear between the two leaves. Stitch an X through all layers of the leaves and pear.

Sweet Pear Ornament
felted sweater scraps in yellow and green

green and yellow roving

yarn

¼" x 2" (6mm x 5cm) wool felt strip

fiberfill

iron and press cloth

scissors

needle

straight pins

Little Bird Ornament
felted sweater scraps

wool felt

double-sided fusible web

fiberfill

curly mohair locks

2 beads

alligator hair clip

sewing machine

felting needle

iron and press cloth

scissors

disappearing-ink marker

fabric glue

straight pins

Oak Leaf Ornament
felted sweater scraps, approx 3" x 5" (8cm x 13cm)

wool felt

cotton print fabric

double-sided fusible web

small felt balls

two horn buttons (20Ligne)

embroidery floss

sewing machine

scissors

chalk liner

needle

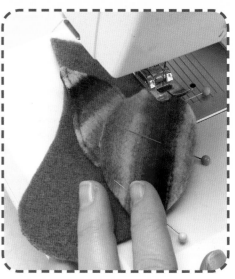

1. Cut out body, wings and beak

Using the templates on page 131, cut out two body pieces (one should be reversed) and one tummy piece from felted sweater scraps. For the bird wings, fuse felted sweater scraps to wool felt with double-sided fusible web. Use the template on page 131 to trace the wings onto one side of each fused wool scrap with a disappearing-ink marker. Trace one wing pattern in reverse. Straight stitch with the sewing machine around wing outlines. Using sharp embroidery scissors, trim out the wing 1/16" (2mm) from the stitching line. Repeat for the other wing. Fuse two small scraps of wool felt together for the beak. Mark the shape using the template on page 131. Straight stitch with the sewing machine around the beak, then cut it out.

2. Edge stitch wings to body

Attach each wing to its respective body piece by stitching on top of the original stitch line just at the front of the wing, leaving the back of the wing unattached.

3. Sew one side of tummy piece

With right sides together, pin and straight stitch the tummy piece to one side of the body.

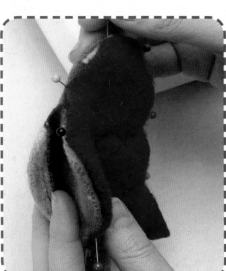

5. Attach eyes and needle felt tuft

Hand-stitch beads onto the bird's face for eyes, and needle felt a tuft of mohair on top of the head.

6. Cut slit and glue clip

Slit sweater felt at the back of the tummy piece for the clip. Apply a dab of glue in the slit and slide in the clip upside down, following the curve of the tummy.

4. Sew, turn and stuff ornament

Pin the beak in place facing inward. Place the other side of the body on top, and with right sides together, pin into place. Stitch with 1/4" (6mm) seam allowance around the entire perimeter, leaving a 1" (3cm) opening at the side of the tummy for turning the work. Trim seam allowances, and clip corners. Turn right-side out and steam press with a press cloth. Stuff with fiberfill and hand stitch it closed.

Oak Leaf Ornament

1. Trace oak leaf pattern onto fused felt

Fuse one scrap of felted sweater to one scrap of printed cotton with fusible web. Fuse a second felted sweater scrap to a scrap of wool felt. Use the pattern on page 131 and a chalk liner to trace a leaf onto each piece of fused fabric onto the side with the best contrast. See Techniques to Learn, pages 14–15, for step-by-step instructions on fusing and appliqué.

2. Cut out sewn leaves

Straight stitch around each leaf outline with a sewing machine. Stitch the leaf vein detail as well. Using sharp embroidery scissors, trim out the leaf 1/16" (2mm) from stitching line. Repeat for the remaining leaf.

3. Attach loop with zigzag stitch

Sandwich the felt loop between the top of the leaves and zigzag stitch it in place.

4. Create acorns

Thread a needle with a length of embroidery floss and tie a knot at one end. Push the needle up through the felt ball and through one of the button's holes. Crisscross the thread through the button holes while catching the top of the felt ball to secure. Exiting from the top of the button, thread the second button onto the needle. Stitch down through a second felt ball, leaving a length of floss between the acorns. Form a French knot (see page 12) on the bottom of the second ball, continuing with the needle up through the ball and button. Crisscross thread through the holes while catching the top of the felt ball to secure. Tie off and clip thread.

5. Tack acorns and bow to oak leaves

Tie a 6" (15cm) length of felt strip into a bow. Tack the bow on top of the leaves, covering the zigzag from the loop. Hand stitch the center of the floss length from the acorns to the top of the leaves, hiding the thread under the bow.

—David Byrne, "Creatures of Love"

little creatures

We all have little creatures in our lives. Why not accentuate their cuteness by outfitting them just right? Fortunately, felted wool can be soft, durable, even washable...perfect for kids, babies and pets. This chapter offers eight whimsical projects to spark your imagination and theirs! Bright colors, soft textures, playful patterns and unexpected embellishments make these projects irresistible and destined to be favorites.

Try the *Haute Dawg Doggie Coat* (see page 60) for the family canine or make the sweet *Baby Blanket* (see page 44) as a gift. Be they beast or babe, someone little is sure to appreciate your efforts.

After all, it's their job to be cute...and not just when they are sleeping.

BRIGHT IDEA

Did you know that wool naturally repels moisture? Whenever, um, "spit happens," your blanket can be kept stain free by simply brushing off the "spill." And if the blanket does require a washing, hand-wash or machine wash it in cold water inside a zippered pillowcase.

baby blanket

materials

3 or 4 felted sweaters cut into 6 10" x 10" (25cm x 25cm) squares and 6 10" x 6" (25cm x 15cm) rectangles

1 yd (1m) prewashed cotton flannel, 45" (114cm) wide

yarn

embroidery floss and needle

wool roving

sewing machine

scissors

pencil

rotary cutter and mat

iron and press cloth

felting needles and foam pad (or Clover needle-felting tool and mat, as shown)

tapestry needle

straight pins

Look no further for the perfect baby gift. You'll be a hit at the next shower with this unique blanket any new mother will love for her little one. Personalize it with a needle-felted monogram and cuddly critter.

Backed with cotton flannel, this project is the perfect weight to keep baby warm through winter as a stroller blanket or to keep him or her happy in a cozy spot for tummy time. Super soft and even washable, this whimsical patchwork baby blanket is sure to achieve "lovey" status and be cherished for years.

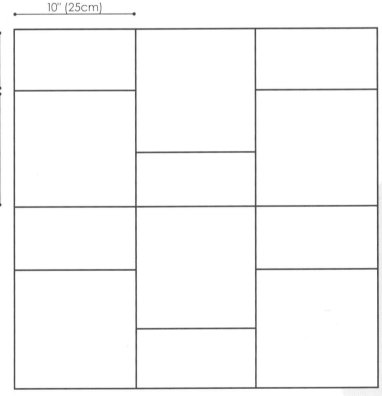

Follow this diagram to make a blanket like the one pictured, or make up your own.

tip

Number each square of the blanket with pieces of masking tape to help you remember your layout once you start assembling the blanket.

1. Arrange squares and rectangles for blanket

Cut felted sweater bodies into six 10" (25cm) squares. Cut smaller felted sweater pieces (sleeves) into six 10" x 6" (25cm x 15cm) rectangles. Use the pattern on page 132 to cut out two pocket shapes, utilizing a finished edge, such as a ribbing, for the top of each pocket. Arrange the squares and rectangles into three columns, alternating between squares and rectangles. You may follow the layout as shown, or create your own.

2. Felt rectangle of roving

Lay out a 4" (10cm) area of roving on a needle-felting bristle brush, layering the fibers vertically and horizontally. Needle felt the roving into a matted rectangle.

3. Cut out turtle from felted roving

Use the pattern on page 132 to cut out the turtle (or desired animal or letter) and pin the template on top of the needle-felted wool. Cut around the shape to create the turtle's body.

4. Needle felt turtle to pocket

Place one of the pockets on top of the felting mat and needle felt the turtle to the pocket.

5. Embellish turtle

Trace the shell pattern on page 132 and cut it out. Needle felt a rectangle of brown roving and cut out the turtle's shell from the needle-felted roving, as for the turtle's body. Lay out some loose roving in a swirl on the turtle's shell. Needle felt the swirl into place. Remove the turtle from the mat, cover it with a press cloth and steam it briefly. Using embroidery needle and floss, make two French knots (see page 12) for eyes. If desired, repeat the needle-felting process to add a letter to the remaining pocket.

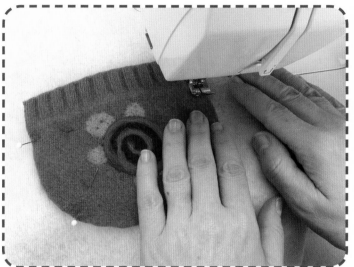

6. Sew pockets onto blanket squares

Pin each pocket to a blanket square and edge stitch around each one, leaving the tops open.

7. Seam squares together into columns

With right sides together, seam the squares and rectangles of the first column together, leaving a ¼" (6mm) seam allowance. (See Techniques to Learn, page 12, for a close-up of straight stitch.) Steam press all seams open from the wrong side. Repeat for the remaining two columns. Seam the three columns together. Steam press all seams open from the wrong side. Trim corners of seam allowances at cross seams. Thread a tapestry needle with a double strand of yarn. Stitch Xs at seam intersections as desired.

8. Trim backing fabric

Spread a piece of cotton flannel for the backing of the blanket face up on your cutting surface. Place the patchwork front of the blanket face down on top of the backing fabric so that right sides are together. Pin the pieces together. Trim the flannel, following the edge of the patchwork front.

9. Finish blanket with edge stitch

Stitch the front and back of the blanket together, sewing ¼" (6mm) from the edge, leaving a 6" (15cm) opening for turning right side out. Trim all corners and seam allowances at intersecting seams. Turn the work right-side out through the opening and steam press it from the flannel side. Turn in the seam allowance at the opening and baste it closed. Finish the blanket with edge stitching around the perimeter, about ⅛" (3mm) from the edge.

little girl's teacup jumper

materials

When designing for little girls, it's important to keep clothes both fashionable and functional (think jump rope and hanging upside down from the monkey bars). In this design, the free-moving A-line shape and easy-on shoulder buttons will get the little girl in your life dressed lickety-split. The pretty teacup pocket offers a place for special treasures or even a tiny friend, such as this curious mousie finger puppet.

Be playful with your color choices and pattern mixing. Line the jumper with a soft cotton print that pulls it all together. But be prepared, because once you make the first one, you're sure to have every little girl at playgroup asking for her own!

- felted sweaters
- 1 yd (91cm) cotton print fabric for lining
- wool felt scraps
- double-sided fusible web
- trim (such as rickrack)
- yarn
- thread
- 2 seed beads (for Mousie eyes)
- buttons
- needle
- sewing machine
- iron and press cloth
- scissors
- pencil
- straight pins

sizes

	2T	3T	4T
Length from Shoulder	17½" (44cm)	19" (48cm)	20½" (52cm)
Chest	26" (66cm)	27" (69cm)	28" (71cm)

-TEMPLATE-
Teacup Appliqué

Teacup appliqué shown at actual size.

tip

Lining should be a smooth-faced fabric without a nap, such as a plain-weave cotton. For ease of construction, the lining hangs free, only attached at the top of the garment. If her lining rides up, hand tack the jumper to the lining at the side seams.

1. Lay out pieces for jumper and make lining

Use the templates on pages 133–134 to cut out the pattern for the jumper in the size you want. Cut pieces of felted sweaters and arrange them to make the jumper front and back. Also use the full pattern to cut out two pieces of printed cotton for the lining. Sew the lining front and back together along the sides. Trim and finish the seam allowances to prevent fraying. Hem the lining, finishing the raw edge and turning up ½" (1cm) total.

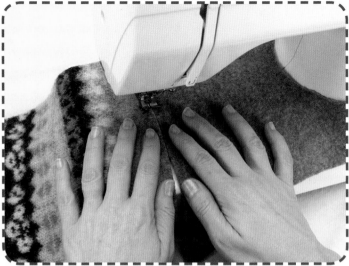

2. Zigzag stich jumper pieces together

Butt together the edges of the sweater pieces for the front and back of the jumper. Zigzag stitch (4W, 2.5L) all patchwork seams. Steam press the finished front and back from the wrong side. See Techniques to Learn, page 12, for a close-up of zigzag stitch.

3. Attach heart and teacup appliqués

Trace the handle and saucer shapes (see page 49) in reverse onto double-sided fusible web, and fuse them to the wrong side of a felt piece. Trim them out. Trace the cup (see page 49) onto felt and cut it out. *Do not* apply double-sided fusible web to the back. Lay out the placement of the saucer and handle on the front of the jumper. Remove the paper backing and fuse them into place while covering them with a press cloth. Zigzag stitch (W3, L2.5) the edge of the saucer and handle. Embellish the cup as desired with trim and a needle-felted heart. Pin the cup pocket into place. Straight stitch ⅛" (3mm) in from the edge, and then zigzag stitch (W3, L2.5) around the edge, leaving the top edge unstitched for the pocket opening. See Techniques to Learn, pages 14–15 for step-by-step instructions on fusing and appliqué.

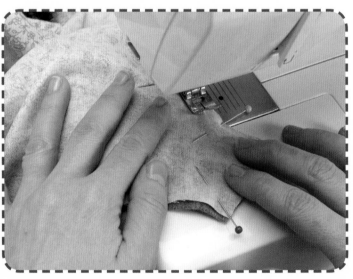

4. Straight stitch side seams and attach lining

With right sides together, straight stitch the side seams of the jumper, leaving ⅜" (10mm) seam allowances. (See Techniques to Learn, page 12, for a close-up of straight stitch.) Press the seams open from the wrong side and trim. Hem the bottom edge of the jumper. Turn the hem under ½" (1cm) and straight stitch the edge on the machine. With right sides together, pin the lining to the jumper at the neck and armholes. Straight stitch ⅛" (3mm) in from the edge. Trim the corners and clip the curves. Turn the entire garment right side out, working out the corners of the straps. Steam press from the lining side of the garment. Edge stitch ⅛" (3mm) in from the edge around the neck and armholes. Steam press from the lining side. Mark and make button holes on the front of the jumper, then sew buttons to the back straps.

Mousie Finger Puppet

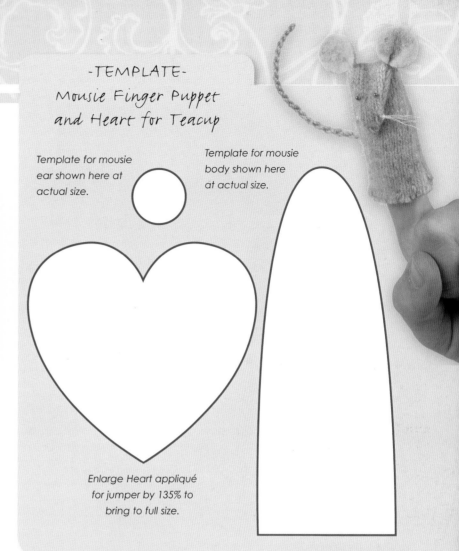

Template for mousie ear shown here at actual size.

Template for mousie body shown here at actual size.

Enlarge Heart appliqué for jumper by 135% to bring to full size.

1. Create body of mouse and stitch nose

Using the pattern on this page, cut the front and back of the mouse out of sweater felt. With right sides together, straight stitch the edges together, leaving a ⅛" (3mm) seam allowance. Turn the mouse right-side out and steam press it, covering it with a press cloth. Fold the top down 1" (3cm) and stitch the "nose" to the front with a yarn accent.

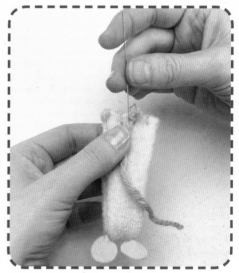

2. Hand stitch felt ears to mouse

Cut two circles out of felt for the mouse ears. Fold each circle in half and hand stitch it to the corner of the head. Repeat for the other ear.

3. Twist yarn to form tail

Cut a 24" (61cm) length of yarn, and fold the yarn in half. Hold the folded end of the yarn in one hand and twist the free ends with the other hand. Twist the yarn until it doubles back on itself. Tie off the end of the yarn so the tail measures 5" (13cm).

4. Attach eyes and tail and finish bottom edge

Hand-stitch the bead eyes and yarn tail to the mouse body. You can also add whiskers, if you'd like. Blanket stitch around the bottom edge of the mouse with yarn.

boy's robot vest

materials

felted sweaters,
including rib trim

wool craft felt

double-sided fusible web

buttons, washers, gears, etc.

embroidery floss

monofilament plastic thread

sewing machine

needle

iron and press cloth

scissors

pencil

straight pins

Sizes
See page 136 for sizing information.
Sizes given for 12 mos through 4T.

Boys are us! My two little boys love refashioned sweaters, especially when they get to pick the colors and the character on the front. Using the same pattern, you can create different outfits for your kids by varying the appliqué design. Think out of the box when embellishing your appliqué. The small washers, gears and O-rings on this vest are extra robot-y. Be sure to attach them firmly and turn the garment inside out for laundering. (For kids less than three years old, be on the safe side. Forgo tack-ons and stick with embroidered embellishment only.)

Since you begin with a shrunken adult-sized sweater, utilize details such as ribbings when cutting out the new garment. For this vest, the bottom edge of the vest pattern was placed along the original sweater's waist ribbing. Doing this saves time and results in a more finished look.

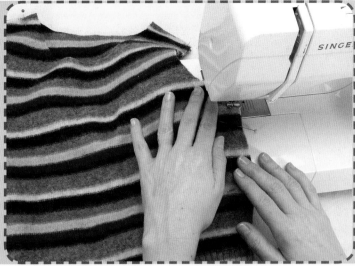

1. Cut out pieces

Using the patterns on pages 136–137, cut out the front and back of the vest in the size you want. Cut ribbed pieces of felted sweaters for the trim for the armholes, neckline and waist according to armhole, waist and neckline dimensions on the full-size pattern. (Or utilize the finished part of the felted sweater for the bottom of the vest.) Cut two 15" (38cm) x 1½" (4cm) pieces of ribbing for the armholes, cut one 17" (43cm) x 1½" (4cm) piece of ribbing for the neckline, and cut one 24" (61cm) x 2" (5cm) piece of ribbing for the waistline, if necessary.

2. Sew shoulder seams and side seams

With right sides together, sew the front and back of the vest together at the shoulder seams and side seams. (See Techniques to Learn, page 12, for more information on straight stitch.) Trim the seam allowances, and steam press the vest from the wrong side.

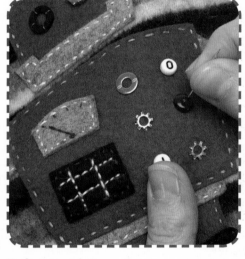

3. Sew rib together to form a circle

Sew together the ends of each ribbed piece for the armhole ribbing to create a circle. Repeat for the neckline.

4. Sew ribbing to vest to form armholes, neckline

With right sides together, pin the armhole ribbing to one armhole, making sure the ribbing seam lines up with the underarm seam of the vest. Distribute the fabric evenly as you pin. Sew the ribbing to the vest armhole, leaving a ¼" (6mm) seam allowance. Repeat for the other armhole and the neckline. Turn the vest right side out. Steam the armhole and neckline seams lightly.

5. Create robot

Trace robot motifs (see page 135) in reverse onto the paper side of double-sided fusible web. Fuse each robot part to desired color of wool felt. Cut out shapes. Peel paper backing off and lay out design on sweater front. (See Techniques to Learn, pages 14–15, for step-by-step instructions on fusing and appliqué.) Take care to center. Overlap robot pieces when fusing together—there shouldn't be any space between pieces. Cover the appliqué with a press cloth and steam fuse it as per the web directions. Using three strands of embroidery floss, stitch around each shape, adding details as desired. As a finishing touch, sew on buttons, washers and other doodads as desired. If you'd like to use washers (as shown), use a clear monofilament thread to stitch them in place.

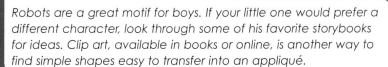

BRIGHT IDEA

Robots are a great motif for boys. If your little one would prefer a different character, look through some of his favorite storybooks for ideas. Clip art, available in books or online, is another way to find simple shapes easy to transfer into an appliqué.

poncho loco

Girls love the novelty of a poncho. It's the perfect combination of style and comfort, and it feels like wearing a great big hug. Put it on as a layering piece or as a light jacket. Its swingy shape has instant twirl appeal!

Blanket-stitch edging and felt-ball dangles give this style plenty of personality. For even more girlie embellishment, add the sweet flower brooch.

materials

2 or 3 felted sweaters, including rib trim
accent yarn
felt balls
sewing machine
iron and press cloth
fabric glue
straight pins
pin back (optional)

tip

Whenever you stitch across an intersecting seam, backstitch for strength.

sizes

Make two rectangles measuring a total of:	S (3–4T)	M (5–6)	L (7–8)
	10" (25cm) x 22" (56cm)	12" (30cm) x 24" (61cm)	14" (36cm) x 26" (66cm)

-TEMPLATE-
Flower Brooch

Templates for flower brooch shown here at actual size.

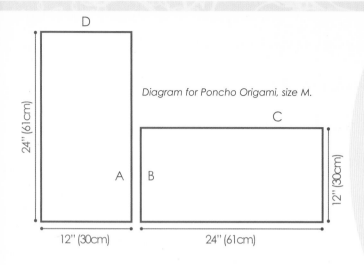

Diagram for Poncho Origami, size M.

D

24" (61cm)

A   B

C

12" (30cm)

12" (30cm)   24" (61cm)

tip This design, while simple in construction, will exercise your spatial reasoning with two "origami" folds that transform two flat rectangles into a three-dimensional garment.

1. Create rectangles

Seam pieces of felted sweaters together using the zigzag technique to create two 12" x 24" (30cm x 61cm) rectangles. (See Techniques to Learn, page 12, for a close-up of zigzag stitch.) To duplicate the project as shown, cut eight 6" x 12" (15cm x 30cm) rectangles. Zigzag stitch them together as illustrated in the diagram on this page. Backstitch at intersecting seams. Arrange the two 12" x 24" (30cm x 61cm) rectangles so that sides A and B align (see diagram on this page).

2. Fold and seam into poncho shape

Fold the poncho according to the diagram so that the free short end (D) lines up with the other side of the poncho (C). Zigzag stitch side A to side B and side C to side D.

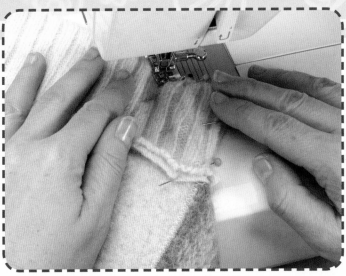

3. Sew on first half of neckline ribbing

Cut two pieces of ribbing approximately 1½" to 2" (4cm to 5cm) wide and 12" (30cm) long. With right sides facing, straight stitch one piece of ribbing to the neckline, center front to center back, leaving a ¼" (6mm) seam allowance. (See Techniques to Learn, page 12, for a close-up of straight stitch.) Repeat with the remaining ribbed piece for the other side of the neckline.

4. Miter front and back of neckline ribbing

Steam press the seam allowances toward the body of the garment. With the poncho wrong-side out, pin the excess rib at the center front, mitering the ends. Stitch the seam at a 45° angle. Repeat for the center back of the neckline. Trim the excess rib to ¼" (6mm), then press from the wrong side.

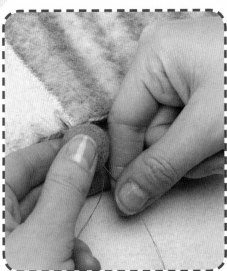

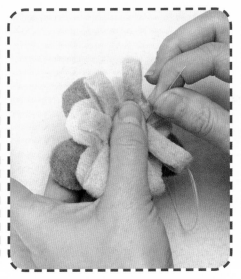

5. Blanket stitch and add felt balls

With yarn, hand blanket stitch around the bottom edge the of poncho. (See Techniques to Learn, page 13, for instructions on blanket stitch.) Stitch an X at the piecing intersections, if desired. Add felt balls along the hem as a final embellishment, if desired.

6. Begin brooch (optional)

Fold a 3" x 5" (8cm x 13cm) piece of felt in half lengthwise and seam one long side. Snip the folded side at ¼" (6mm) intervals (see *Breakfast-in-Bed Pillow*, page 30, for more information). Bend the snipped piece into a circle, and sew the ends together. Cut out two flowers in complementary colors using the template on page 55. Layer the flowers, and sew the petal circle into place. Glue a felt ball in the center of the flower.

7. Finish flower brooch

Use the template provided on page 55 to make a leaf. Cut two small slits in the leaf to accommodate the pin back. The distance between the slits should equal the length of the pin back. Slide a pin back through the slits. Glue the flower to the leaf with fabric glue, covering the pin back.

tween hooded scarf

materials

- 2 or 3 felted sweaters
- accent yarn
- 7 pompoms (or yarn to make them)
- sewing machine
- scissors
- straightedge
- chalk liner
- straight pins

You've seen them...those big kids walking to school in the winter with no hats, coats unzipped, flapping in the breeze. Brrr, it makes me cold just looking at them. I guess being warm wasn't cool. Until now!

The *Tween Hooded Scarf* is a super-quick project for the style-conscious young person. It can be made to coordinate (read: "blend") with other outerwear or it can be bold and shout out rebellion. No hat to lose along the way, it's all attached, a two-in-one combo. With just a few soft wool sweaters and a little sewing, all the angst-ridden issues of youth are resolved. Well, we can dream...

1. Sew hood

Cut two sides of the hood out of felted sweaters using the pattern on page 138 (reverse one piece). Sew the center seam of the hood, leaving a ¼" (6mm) seam allowance. Turn back a ¼" (6mm) hem at the front edge of the hood and straight stitch. Press seams from the wrong side. See Techniques to Learn, page 12, for more information on straight stitch.

2. Cut top scarf pieces at 45° angle

Cut six rectangles 6" (15cm) wide, and long enough to create two scarf sides to reach your desired length. (Each of my six rectangles is about 13" [33cm] long.) Arrange the pieces in the order you like. Layer the two top pieces, one on top of the other. Place a straightedge at an angle on top of the layered pieces. Mark and cut a 45° angle across the top edge of both rectangles. These edges will be attached to the hood. (Do not cut angles on remaining rectangles.)

3. Sew angled pieces to hood

With right sides together, pin and straight stitch the angled edges to the bottom edges of the hood. (The point of the angle should align with the center back of the hood.) Press the seam allowances down (toward scarf) and edge stitch downward to secure them. With right sides together, pin and straight stitch the remaining rectangles together to create two lengths of scarf.

4. Sew on pompoms

Make seven pompoms, one large and six small. Sew the large pompom to the center top of the hood, and sew three pompoms evenly spaced at each scarf end.

There are many gadgets available in craft stores for making pompoms. You can also make your own tool with two round pieces of cardboard. They should measure 1" (3cm) bigger in diameter than you want the pompom to be. Cut holes in the center of both circles and place them one on top of the other. Using multiple strands, wrap yarn from the center to the edge and back through the center again. Continue wrapping yarn, distributing it evenly around the circle. Insert the blade of the scissors in between the outside edges of the cardboard circles. Cut yarn evenly around the circle. Pull the cards apart slightly and wrap a length of yarn tightly between the cards (around the middle of the yarn strands) a few times. Secure the yarn tie with a double knot. Adjust and fluff the pompom. Trim away any excess yarn.

Pompom Squad

haute dawg doggie coat

Your family Fido will be strutting his stuff in this stylish yet functional outerwear. Wool is naturally water repellant, so an occasional raindrop will just shed right off—it's great for those misty morning walks.

This pattern is easily adjusted to fit most small- to medium-sized dogs. Use two or three felted sweaters, depending on the size of your pooch. Simply measure around the dog's chest behind his front legs. Divide that number by two, then add 2" (5cm). Enlarge the pattern on page 132 to equal that measurement. Hot dog appliqué shown here with I-cord mustard...add your own canine condiments as desired.

materials

- lightweight felted sweaters in 2 colors
- wool felt (optional)
- double-sided fusible web
- felted I-cord worked in gold yarn
- Velcro strips, 4" (10cm) total
- fabric glue
- sewing machine
- iron and press cloth
- needle and thread
- disappearing-ink marker
- scissors
- pencil
- straight pins

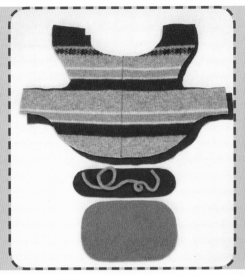

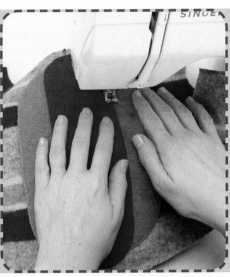

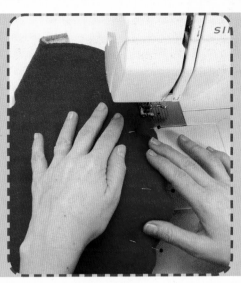

1. Cut out pattern pieces

Size the pattern according to the size of the dog you're making it for. Use the pattern on page 132 to cut out one piece for the coat and one for the lining. Trace the hot dog and bun appliqué design onto the paper side of sheets of double-sided fusible web. Fuse the dog and the bun to appliqué fabric (wool felt or felted sweater), and cut out the shapes (see templates on page 137).

2. Fuse bun and hot dog to coat

Place the bun appliqué on the center back of the outer coat and fuse it into place. (See Techniques to Learn, pages 14–15, for step-by-step instructions on fusing and appliqué.) Zigzag stitch along the edge with matching thread. Repeat with the hot dog.

3. Seam lining to coat

With right sides together, pin and sew the outer coat to the lining, leaving a 3" (8cm) opening to turn the piece right-side out.

BRIGHT IDEA

Think of other appliqué designs that might suit your dog's personality. How about a green pea pod with the little green peas sewn up the center for your little "sweet pea"? Maybe a banana split: Make two yellow banana shapes with "scoops" of chocolate, strawberry and vanilla ice cream appliqués on top!

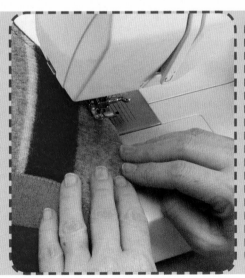

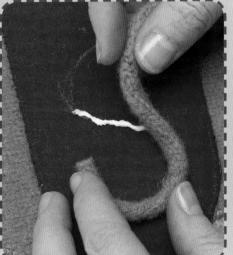

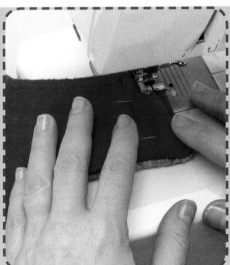

4. Edge stitch along perimeter of coat

Trim and clip the seam allowances. Turn the coat right-side out and steam press it. With needle and thread, hand stitch the opening closed. Edge stitch around the entire perimeter of the coat.

5. Adhere mustard to hot dog

Mark the placement of the I-cord "mustard" with disappearing-ink marker or chalk marker. Apply a thin bead of fabric glue along the marked line. Place the I-cord along the glue bead, and let it dry. Hand stitch the I-cord into place.

6. Attach Velcro closures

Cut Velcro into 2" (5cm) strips. Pin the Velcro onto the neck and chest tabs. Machine stitch around the edges of the Velcro tabs to secure them.

sunflower kitty nap-n-play

Oh, the enviable life of a cat: snoozing in sunbeams on lazy afternoons, playing with yarn, generally being adorable. We humans could never get away with that! On the upside, we do have opposable thumbs and the ability to make things.

The *Sunflower Kitty Nap-n-Play* is designed to give your pet a soft and special place to curl up while giving you something fun to make and pretty to look at. The flower center is padded with quilt batting for extra cushioning. But when kitty rouses from her slumber, the tethered ladybug toy awaits for some frisky playtime.

materials

felted sweaters in compatible colors

batting

approx 25" (64cm) felted I-cords worked in colors to accent the sweater colors

yarn

wool roving (for spots on ladybug's wings)

fiberfill

sewing machine

scissors

disappearing-ink marker or chalk liner

needle-felting tools

tapestry needle

straight pins

fabric glue

Templates for Ladybug Toy shown at actual size.

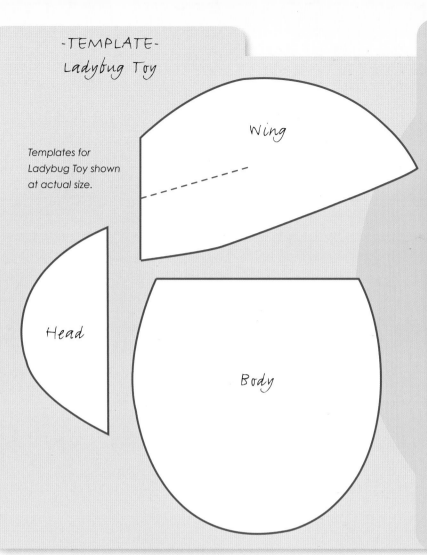

Wing

Head

Body

1. Pin top felt circle to batting

Cut two circles 12½" (32cm) in diameter out of felted sweater for the front and back center of the flower bed (see template, page 138). Cut two layers of batting the same size. Pin the front felted sweater circle to the two layers of batting.

2. Mark swirl with chalk liner

Machine stitch the batting and the top felt circle together around the circumference. Mark the spiral design with a disappearing-ink marker or a chalk liner. Machine stitch through all layers along the marked spiral line.

3. Hand stitch over sewn spiral

Hand stitch with contrasting yarn (running stitch) and tapestry needle on top of the machine stitching.

4. Zigzag stitch I-cord to petals

Cut six orange and six green petals out of felted sweater scraps using the pattern on page 138. Apply I-cord to the long edge of each petal using a zigzag stitch.

5. Pin and sew orange petals

With right sides together, pin the orange petals around the perimeter of the flower center. Straight stitch them in place using the sewing machine, leaving a ¼" (6mm) seam allowance. See Techniques to Learn, page 12, for a close-up of straight stitch.

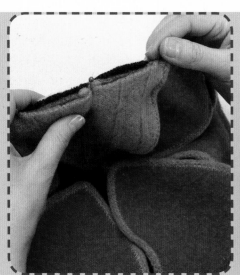

6. Pin and sew green petals

Pin the green petals around the perimeter of the flower center, offsetting them to fall between the orange petals. Straight stitch them in place with the sewing machine.

7. Whipstitch I-cord onto front

Run a bead of fabric glue around the circumference of the center circle where the petals are joined. Push the fuchsia I-cord firmly into the glue, then let it dry. Whipstitch around the I-cord with a contrasting (gold) yarn.

8. Secure backing

Turn the mat over and run another bead of fabric glue around the outer edge of the batting. Place the "back" of the flower center on top. After the glue dries, trim away any excess and whipstitch the edge closed with matching thread. Leave a 1" (3cm) opening to attach the cord for the toy.

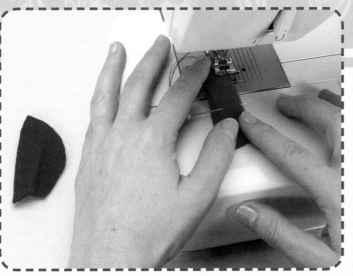

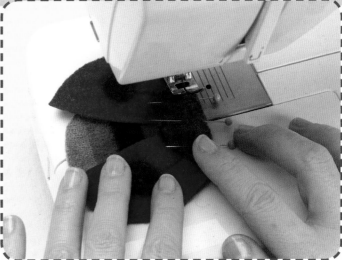

1. Sew tucks in ladybug wings

Cut two of each pattern piece for the ladybug using the patterns on page 63. Fold one wing in half and pin it. Sew ⅛" (3mm) away from the fold line for about 1" (3cm) to create a tuck in the wing. Repeat for the second wing. Needle felt a spot below the tuck (top of the wing) on each wing.

2. Sew wings and head to top of body

With right sides together, place the wings across the top edge of the top piece of the body. Layer the head on top, sandwiching the wings. Stitch across the seam. Open the seam and press it flat. With right sides together, place bottom head on top of bottom body. Stitch across the seam. Press the seam flat.

3. Stitch ladybug top and bottom together

Tie a knot at one end of a length of red I-cord, then measure up about 2" (5cm) and tie another knot. Cut the I-cord about ⅛" (3mm) above this second knot. Bend the knotted I-cord in half and sandwich it between the ladybug bottom and ladybug top so the "U" of the antennae sticks out of the top. Pin the antennae and ladybug sides in place. Tuck in the wings so they don't get caught in the seams. Stitch around the perimeter of the ladybug, leaving 1" (3cm) open at the hind end for turning.

4. Finish ladybug

Turn the ladybug right-side out. Stuff her with fiberfil. Insert one end of the I-cord tether (12" to 18" [30cm to 46cm]) into the opening and hand-stitch the opening closed.

5. Sew tether to cat bed

Slip the other end of the I-cord tether into the opening you left in the bottom of the backing and hand-stitch it in place.

hand puppets

Pugsly the Pug is an expressive dog. His tousled ears reveal his devil-may-care attitude. Smitten the Kitten is all about love. Giddy like a schoolgirl with gleaming button eyes, she never stops purring.

These puppets are as fun to make as they are to play make-believe with. Felted scraps in natural colors and brights alike work well for these characters. Minimal embroidery adds the right touch and gets them finished fast.

Make this odd couple a pair at your own risk, for they may fight like…well, cats and dogs.

felted sweater scraps
wool craft felt
double-sided fusible web
embroidery floss
buttons
sewing machine
iron and press cloth
scissors
needle
straight pins

Pugsly the Pug

1. Sew tuck to form muzzle

Cut out all the pieces for Pugsly from felted sweater scraps using the patterns on pages 139–140. Cut the front, back and head out of one color sweater. Cut the muzzle and ears from a second color. Use red wool felt for the nose and lighter felt for the eyeballs. Fuse the red nose to the center of Pugsly's muzzle. Straight stitch the center-front notch on Pugsly's muzzle by folding the muzzle in half with right sides together.

2. Attach eyes and zigzag seam muzzle

Fuse the eye shapes onto Pugsly's face with fusible web (see Fuisng in the Techniques to Learn section, page 14). Mark the center front of Pugsly's face with a straight pin. Mark the center of the muzzle in the same way. Butt the two pieces together, using the centered pins as a guide. Zigzag seam the muzzle to the face. See Techniques to Learn, page 12, for a close-up of zigzag stitch.

3. Sew on eyes and blanket stitch around nose

Stitch buttons on top of the eye shapes. Use pink embroidery floss to embellish the nose with a blanket stitch border. See Techniques to Learn, page 13, for instructions on blanket stitch.

4. Sew tucks to create ears

Fold an ear in half and pin it in place. Sew up from the bottom for about 1" (3cm) to create a tuck.

5. Attach ears

Pin the ears onto Pugsly's face, with the ears pointing downward toward the nose. With right sides together, layer the back of the puppet on the face, sandwiching the ears in between. Pin the pieces in place and seam them together. Trim the seam allowances. See Techniques to Learn, page 12, for information on straight stitch.

6. Sew side seams

With right sides together, pin the lower front to the back. Sew the side seam, starting from the bottom edge and ending ¼" (6mm) past the forehead seam. Trim the seam allowances.

  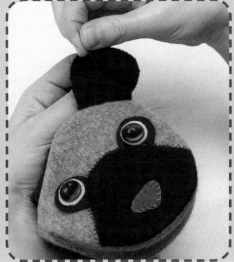

7. Attach tongue to mouth pieces

Cut a tongue out of sweater scraps or wool craft felt. Center the tongue on one of the mouth pieces and sandwich it in between the right sides of the top and bottom of the mouth. Pin the pieces in place and seam them together. Trim the seam allowances.

8. Attach mouth piece to Pugsly's face

With right sides together, pin the top of the mouth to the face and pin the bottom mouth to the puppet front. Stitch the mouth in place with the puppet-side up and the mouth-side down on the machine. Turn Pugsly right-side out and steam press the seams.

9. Sew additional tucks in ear

Fold down the tip of each ear and hand-tack it to create a jaunty angle.

Smitten the Kitten

To make Smitten the Kitten, use the patterns on pages 139–140 and follow the instructions for creating Pugsly the Pug. To finish, give the kitten's eyes an extra layer of felt. Embroider the muzzle notch with chain stitch and add French knot whiskers for a more feline detail.

"Candy on the beach, there's nothing better.
But I like candy when it's wrapped in a sweater."

sweet stuff

What is it about the vibrant colors and delicious feel of felted wool that makes me think of candy? I find it to be pure inspiration. Sweet Stuff is full of delectable projects designed to tickle your fancy and make your mouth water. High fiber and super sweet, you'll want to make these projects to give as gifts to all your sassy, stylish friends.

Whether it's the colorful *Cupcake Pincushions* (see page 72) or the *Ice Cream Cone Tape Measure* (see page 76), these projects are designed to be functional while providing maximum eye candy.

cupcake pincushions

materials

felted sweaters or large sweater scraps in 2 or 3 different colors

1 color felted sweater ribbing

fabric glue (clear drying)

8" to 12" (20cm to 30cm) trim, such as rickrack

small felt ball

scrap of green craft felt for leaf

sewing pins with multicolored pearl heads

scissors

needle and thread

straight pins

Swirls of felted frosting are wrapped in a delicately trimmed cuff and topped with a pink cherry and pearly sprinkles. Something off the dessert menu? No, it's the mega-popular *Cupcake Pincushion*! Inspired by a scrap pile of beautifully colored sweater ribbing and a catnap with my toddler, the idea literally came to me in a dream.

Here's the recipe and all the tips you'll need to make your very own. Use scraps from your brightest felted sweaters to make colorful cupcakes or choose rich brown felt for a "chocolate" fix. Keep it in your sewing basket as a yummy-looking pincushion or display it as a faux food work of art. It also makes a thoughtful birthday gift for anyone who loves to sew or loves cupcakes!

1. Fold rectangles in half and pin
Cut two pieces of felted wool in coordinating colors into rectangles measuring approximately 5" x 10" (13cm x 25cm). (The length of the rectangles depends on the thickness of felt—see Step 3.) Fold each rectangle lengthwise and secure the folded piece with pins inserted perpendicular to the cut edges.

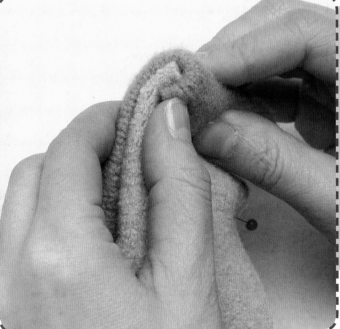

2. Roll rectangles together
Lay one rectangle on top of the other, lining up their folds and offsetting the top rectangle by about ½" (1cm) to the left. Starting at the right end, roll the two rectangles together, stretching the fabric gently as you roll.

3. Trim away excess fabric

Continue rolling the fabric until the diameter of the roll equals about 2½" (6cm). Trim away the excess, and secure the roll with pins.

4. Hand baste roll to secure

Hand baste the ends of the fabric to secure the roll, and remove the pins. Trim any unevenness so the bottom of the roll is flat.

5. Measure and cut ribbing for cupcake wrapper

Measure the ribbing piece by wrapping it around the basted roll. Add ¼" (6mm) to the circumference, and trim the ribbing to size. The height of the rib should equal the height of the roll plus ½" (1cm), about 3" (8cm) total.

6. Baste cupcake sleeve to roll

With right sides together, stitch the ends of the rib together, leaving a ⅛" (3mm) seam allowance. Slide the ribbed sleeve onto the cupcake roll, making sure the raw edge is about ½" (1cm) down from the top of the cupcake. (The finished edge from the original sweater will end up at the bottom of the cupcake.) Hand baste the cupcake sleeve to the top of the roll.

7. Flip cupcake sleeve down

Turn the ribbed sleeve right-side out, rolling it down to cover the roll.

8. Glue scrap to bottom of cupcake

Cut a scrap of felt that matches the ribbing to be used as the bottom of the pincushion. Apply fabric glue around the bottom of the roll up to the ribbed edge. Invert the cupcake and place it on top of the felt bottom. Allow the glue to dry.

9. Trim around cupcake bottom

Using the bottom of the cupcake as a guide, trim around the piece to make a circle.

10. Adhere trim

Measure the circumference of the pincushion around the ribbed cupcake wrapper and cut a piece of trim to that length. Apply a small bead of glue ¼" (6mm) from the top ribbed edge and attach the trim. Pin the trim to hold it in place until it's dry.

11. Adhere cherry

Open the center top of the roll slightly, separating the felt with your index finger. Apply glue in the space and press the felt ball into the center of the cupcake.

Mini Cupcakes

12. Stick in leaf pin

Cut a small leaf shape out of felt and attach it to the cupcake beside the cherry with a nondecorative straight pin. Add decorative pearl pins as "sprinkles."

For the mini version, use rectangles measuring approximately 3" x 5" (8cm x 13cm). Trim them in the same manner as the full-size cupcakes, but use smaller-scale trimmings.

ice cream cone tape measure

The element of surprise is yours when this unassuming little ice cream cone softy reveals its true function. Beneath the decorative felt-ball cherry and sprinkle of sparkly beads is a retractable tape measure in disguise. Ever wondered what you can make with those leftover scraps and trimmings? Here it is! Pull the cherry to measure, and squeeze the ice cream to retract.

As fun to use as it is to make, this project whips up in a jiffy and fits nicely in the sewing bag you're about to make.

materials

round retractable tape measure, approx 2" (5cm) in diameter

"ice cream"-colored felted sweater scraps

"cone"-patterned felted sweater scraps

felt ball

5" (13cm) trim, such as rickrack

small amount of yarn

embroidery floss

seed and bugle beads

pinch of fiberfill

scissors

needle and thread

craft glue

straight pins

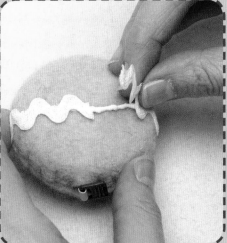

1. Whipstitch tape measure between felt circles

Cut two 2½" (6cm) circles out of "ice cream"-colored felt to create the tape measure cover (see template, page 141). Sandwich the tape measure between the circles, with wrong sides facing the tape measure. Starting on one side of the tape measure opening, whipstitch the edges of the circles together with embroidery floss. After stitching two-thirds of the circumference, stop and stuff a pinch of fiberfill inside the circle on top of the tape measure. Do not stuff the "button" side that retracts the tape measure. (This becomes the back.)

2. Adhere trim

Finish stitching all the way around to the other side of the tape measure opening. Secure the thread. Glue the trim across the front (stuffed side) of the tape measure cover and wrap it around to the back (flat side). Glue it into place with fabric glue. Secure the trim with pins until it dries.

3. Sew and stuff cone

Using the pattern on page 141, cut two cone shapes out of "cone"-patterned sweater felt. Sew both straight sides by hand or machine with right sides together, leaving a ¼" (6mm) seam allowance. Trim excess fabric away from the point of the cone, and turn it right-side out. Stuff the cone with a pinch of fiberfill.

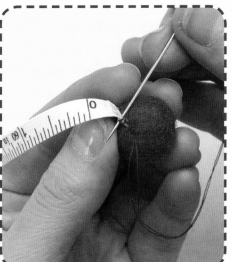
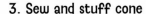

4. Blanket stitch cone to ice cream

Slide the tape measure ice cream into the top of the cone, making sure the tape measure opening is at the top. The cone will cover the bottom edge of the trim. Pin the ice cream into place. Using matching or accent thread, hand-stitch the edge of the cone to the tape measure cover. Be sure to catch all layers securely. For a decorative touch, blanket stitch the edge of the cone using yarn or embroidery floss. See Techniques to Learn, page 13, for instructions on blanket stitch.

5. Adhere felt ball to end of tape measure

Using heavy-duty scissors, cut the plastic tab off the end of the measuring tape. Take care not to retract the end! Using scissors or a sharp craft knife, cut a small slit into the bottom of a ½" (1cm) felt ball. Slide the end of the tape into the slit in the ball and stitch the ball to the end of the tape measure with a needle and matching thread.

6. Sew on sprinkles

Decorate the "ice cream" by sewing seed beads and bugle bead "sprinkles" on top.

77

bonbon journal

What we write in our journals is personal—shouldn't the design be, too? Created to fit a standard-sized blank journal, this project can be customized to fit whatever you've got, be it a journal, sketchbook or any hardcover book. Use bright colors to inspire creativity or calm colors to get you ready to reveal your innermost thoughts. Once the book is filled with your doodles, dreams and aspirations, slide off the removable cover and pop in a new blank book.

These felt-covered journals also make excellent personalized gifts. Try stitching on some alphabet beads to make a quick and thoughtful present.

materials

4" x 6" (10cm x 15cm) hard-bound journal/sketchbook

felted sweater scraps

wool craft felt

double-sided fusible web

1 yd (1m) ¼" (6mm) wide grosgrain ribbon

seed and bugle beads

beading needle

embroidery floss

disappearing-ink marker

sewing machine

iron and press cloth

hole punch

scissors

pinking shears

craft knife and cutting mat

needle

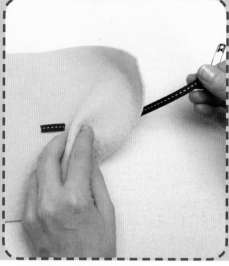

1. Fuse shapes to album cover

Cut two 6½" x 9½" (17cm x 24cm) rectangles, one out of felted sweater and one out of wool craft felt. Using the patterns on page 141, trace bonbon and wrapper shapes onto the paper side of double-sided fusible web. Fuse the shapes to wool felt scraps in desired colors. Cut out the three large wrapper circles with pinking shears. Layer the wrappers and bonbon shapes onto the right edge of the felted sweater rectangle, about ¾" (2cm) from the edge. Cover with a press cloth and fuse them into place. See Techniques to Learn, pages 14–15, for instructions on fusing and appliqué.

2. Add embroidery

For the bottom bonbon, embroider around the perimeter of the wrapper with running stitch. Randomly sew on seed and bugle beads with a beading needle for "sprinkles." For the top bonbon, work in running stitch around the perimeter of the wrapper. Use a hole punch to cut three felt petals for a tiny rose. Stitch the leaves and petals in place, adding a bead in the center. For the center bonbon, work in running stitch around the perimeter of the wrapper. Chain stitch a squiggle on top of the square bonbon. See Techniques to Learn, page 13, for instructions on various embroidery stitches.

3. Thread ribbon through lining

Lay the wool craft felt rectangle onto a cutting mat. Using a craft knife, cut two small slits 1" (3cm) apart at the center of the rectangle. Lace a length of grosgrain ribbon through the slits.

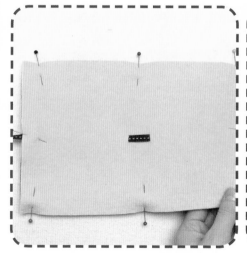

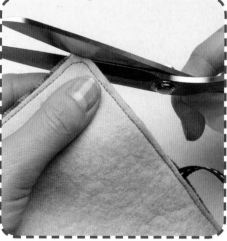

4. Pin lining and cover together

Layer the craft felt lining on top of the wrong side of the embroidered rectangle. Pin around the edges, with the ribbon sandwiched in between. Edge stitch the pieces together, rounding the corners as you come to them.

5. Trim corners

Trim the corners next to the stitch line to round them. Press the pieces from the wool craft felt side.

6. Cut slits for book cover

Measure 3" (8cm) in from the ends on the lining side and mark vertical lines with a disappearing-ink marker. Snip the line at the bottom (carefully, do not poke through the outer layer) and cut smoothly along the line. Repeat for the second line. Take care not to cut the ribbon as you make the slits. Open the journal cover as wide as possible to slip it into the felt cover. Trim the ends of the ribbon to the desired length.

BRIGHT IDEA

Instead of making a ribbon tie, you can create a bookmark by catching a length of ribbon between the cover and the lining at the spine, allowing about 6" (15cm) or so of ribbon to hang over the top. Add a small wool flower at the end of the marker.

cutie pie felt bowls

Sometimes you need a special place to put a little something...your rings, extra buttons, that funny-shaped rock that someone found on the playground. *Cutie Pie Felt Bowls* are the perfect spot for your daily treasures. Inspired by the roly-poly beauty of felt balls, these are simply made with circles and spheres. Two layers of bonded felt wind in and out like pie crust to draw the edges up and create the bowl shape. You can make your own felt balls by hand or purchase them ready-made.

materials

wool craft felt
felted sweater
double-sided fusible web
12 to 14 felt balls
needle and heavy-weight quilter's thread
disappearing-ink marker or chalk liner
iron and press cloth
scissors
straight pins

1. Cut circle from craft felt

Cut a 7" (18cm) circle out of the double-sided fusible web. Fuse it to the wool craft felt, following product directions (see Fusing in the Techniques to Learn section, page 14). Cut the felt out around the edge of the double-sided fusible web. Remove remaining paper.

2. Fuse wool felt circle to sweater felt and cut

Place the web fusible-side down onto the wrong side of a piece of felted sweater. Fuse the craft felt circle to the felted sweater, then trim out the circle. Be sure your work is totally fused around the edges so it doesn't de-laminate once you start working with it. Because the material is so thick, it's best to cover it with a damp press cloth and go back at it with a lot of steam.

3. Arrange felt balls on circle

Place your felt balls around the perimeter to get a feel for how many you'll need. The sample as shown uses fourteen felt balls, alternating between larger balls and smaller ones. Leave about ½" (1cm) between the balls. Make a small mark with disappering-ink marker or chalk liner on the felt to indicate ball placement.

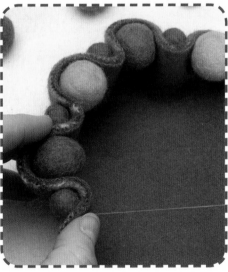

4. Sew felt balls onto circle

Thread a needle with two strands of thread for strength. Starting about ¼" (6mm) from the top edge of the felt, sew through the felt circle, through the center of the first ball, then back through the felt again. Secure the position of each ball with a straight pin. Continue, making sure the felt wraps about halfway around each ball. Following the placement marks, keep adding balls, alternating sides of the felt circle.

5. Check spacing of felt balls

Stop and check about halfway around the circle, making sure you have used half the balls from your estimate.

6. Cinch and tie off thread

Continue working until you're back at the beginning of the circle. After sewing on the last ball, pull the thread taut. When you're happy with the look, remove the pins securing the felt balls and knot the thread in an inconspicuous place.

felted knitting needle case

Every knitter needs a little help now and then. While this project won't help solve the mysteries of a cable twist, the *Felted Knitting Needle Case* provides both organization and inspiration. And we can all use a bit of that! Easy to cut and sew, divided pockets offer plenty of space for needles and accessories of all sizes and shapes. Where better to store your sweater-making tools than in the remnants of an old, loved sweater? Choose a charming Fair Isle pattern or a funky stripe and embellish with a flower appliqué.

materials

felted sweaters
¾ yd (69cm) of wool craft felt
double-sided fusible web
disappearing-ink marker or chalk liner
yarn
13 multicolored buttons
embroidery floss
sewing machine
needle-felting needle and foam pad
iron and press cloth
straight pins

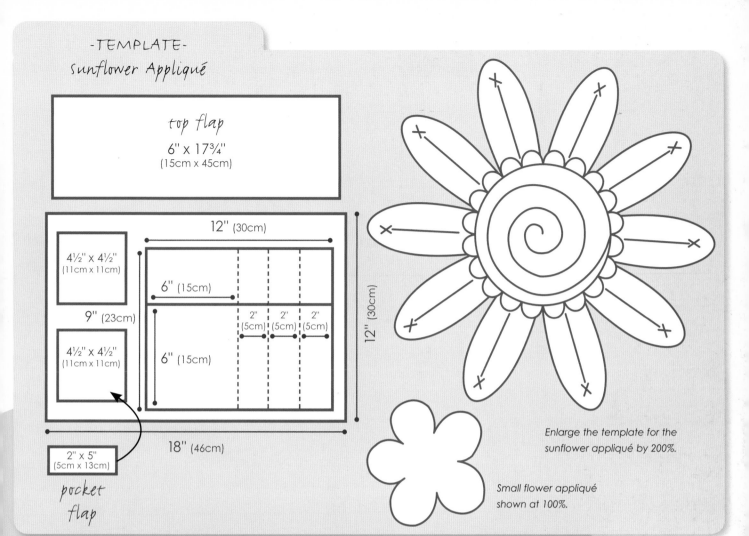

top flap
6" x 17¾"
(15cm x 45cm)

4½" x 4½"
(11cm x 11cm)

9" (23cm)

4½" x 4½"
(11cm x 11cm)

12" (30cm)

6" (15cm)

2"
(5cm)

2"
(5cm)

2"
(5cm)

6" (15cm)

12" (30cm)

18" (46cm)

2" x 5"
(5cm x 13cm)

pocket
flap

Enlarge the template for the
sunflower appliqué by 200%.

Small flower appliqué
shown at 100%.

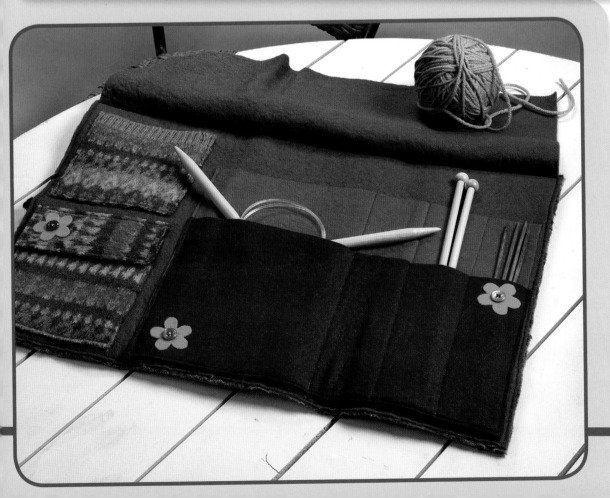

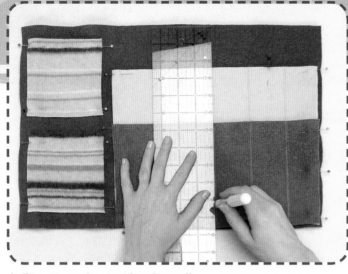

1. Pin pieces for inside of needle case

Place a 12" x 18" (30cm x 46cm) piece of wool craft felt for the lining on your work surface. Layer a 6" x 12" (15cm x 30cm) piece of felt (pictured in dark pink) for the small needle pocket on top of a 9" x 12" (23cm x 30cm) piece of felt (pictured in light pink) for the large pocket. Pin them in place in the bottom right corner of the lining, about ⅛" (3mm) in from the edge of the lining. Also cut two 4½" x 4½" (11cm x 11cm) pockets out of the same felted sweater you're planning to use for the outside of the needle case. If you'd like, utilize the ribbing from a sweater for the top of the top pockets. Pin the pockets in place on the left-hand side of the lining. Using a disappearing-ink marker or a chalk liner, mark vertical lines down the center of the layered large and small pockets. Draw the first line 2" (5cm) in from the right side of the lining. Draw two more lines at 2" (5cm) intervals, measuring from right to left, as shown.

2. Sew down pockets and pocket flap

Edge stitch the sides and bottoms of the large and small pockets to the lining. Stitch down the lines you drew in step 1 to make needle pockets. Also cut out a 2" x 5" (5cm x 13cm) pocket flap and fuse it to a felt sweater scrap. Edge stitch the flap, then stitch it to the lining above the lower pocket. All of the pockets should be stitched in place.

4. Needle felt swirl on flower center

Trace a small circle 3" (8cm) in diameter and a spiral design onto a small square of craft felt with a disappearing-ink marker or chalk liner. Needle felt a single piece of yarn around the spiral design, using one needle (instead of the multiple needles in the felting tool) and a foam pad. Steam press the felt from the wrong side to set the needle felting. Fuse a piece of web to the back. Cut out the circle. See Techniques to Learn, page 16, for more information on needle felting.

3. Fuse flower to outside of case

Cut felted sweaters into a 12" x 18" (30cm x 46cm) rectangle for outer case, zigzag stitching squares and rectangles together if necessary to achieve the total measurement. Use the patterns on page 83 to trace the flower shapes onto double-sided fusible web and fuse the web to the felt pieces. Cut out and fuse the flower shapes to the fabric for the outer case (see photo for placement).

tip

When you're edge stitching around the lining and outer case, backstitch over the tie (where it's sandwiched in place) for extra reinforcement.

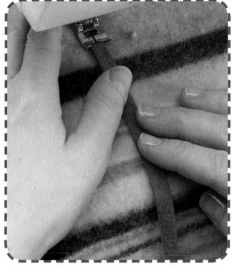

5. Fuse flower in place

Place the flower center on top of the flower and fuse it in place.

6. Embellish flower petals

Pick a contrasting color of floss and embroider up the middle of each petal with running stitch. Stitch on a button at the tip of each petal.

7. Tack one end of tie to case

Cut two strips of felt in a contrasting color to ¼" x 12" (6mm x 30cm). Sew one end of one of the strips to the center of where the case will fold on the outside cover of the needle case, or about 6" (15cm) from the edge.

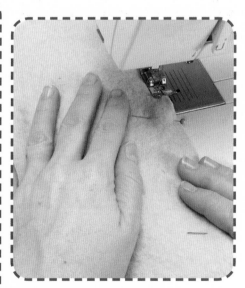

8. Pin and sew lining to outer case

With wrong sides together, pin the lining to the outer case sweater felt rectangle. Sandwich the end of the second tie between the layers where indicated, and pin it in place. Edge stitch the pieces together along the sides and bottom edge.

9. Pin and sew on final flap

Place the top flap (6" x 17¾" [15cm x 45cm]) across the top edge of the lining and pin it in place. Edge stitch through all three layers. (The flap is ¼" [6mm] shorter than the width of the case to accommodate the bulk of the case when folded.)

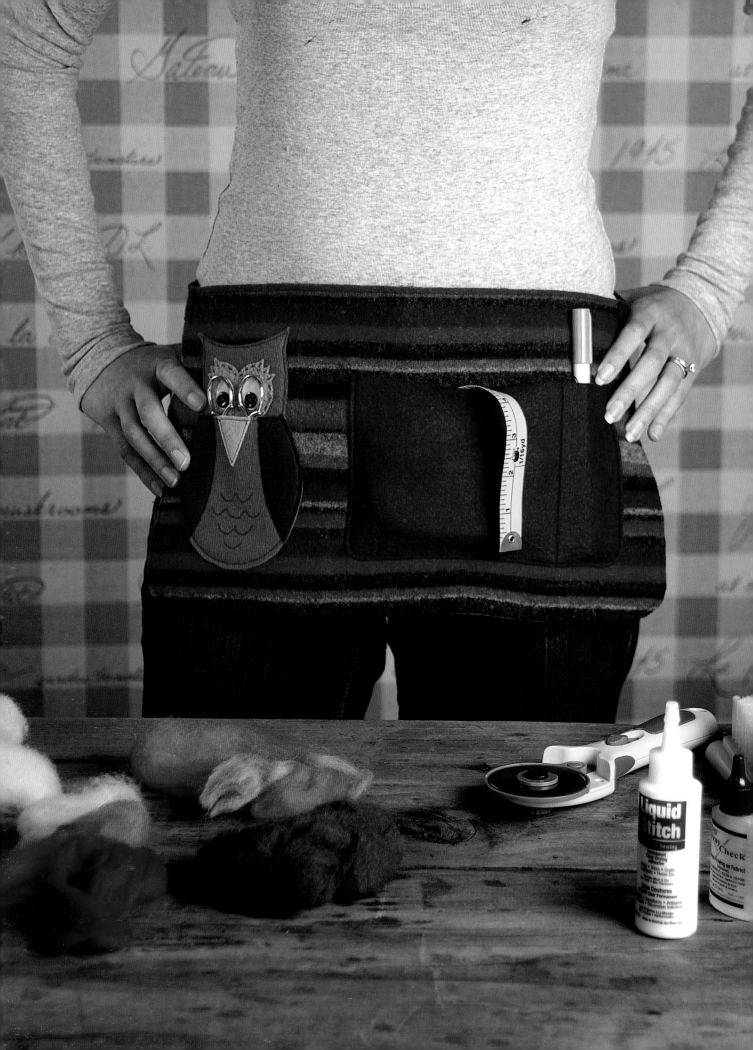

who-has-my-scissors craft apron

materials

"Who has my scissors!?" is a common question around the house. Now we know the answer...Who does! Who, the owl, that is. He'll keep a watchful eye on your work as he peers through the finger holes of your scissors.

Keep your craft and sewing tools close at hand as you move about your craft studio (or craft corner, craft closet, whatever space you have!) with this handy apron. Pockets you can customize and a sassy owl appliqué give you some stylish gear to wear as you get to work.

- felted sweater
- wool craft felt
- double-sided fusible web
- fusible interfacing
- disappearing-ink marker or chalk liner
- 2 small buttons
- needle and embroidery floss
- sewing machine
- scissors
- straight pins

-TEMPLATE-
Owl Appliqué

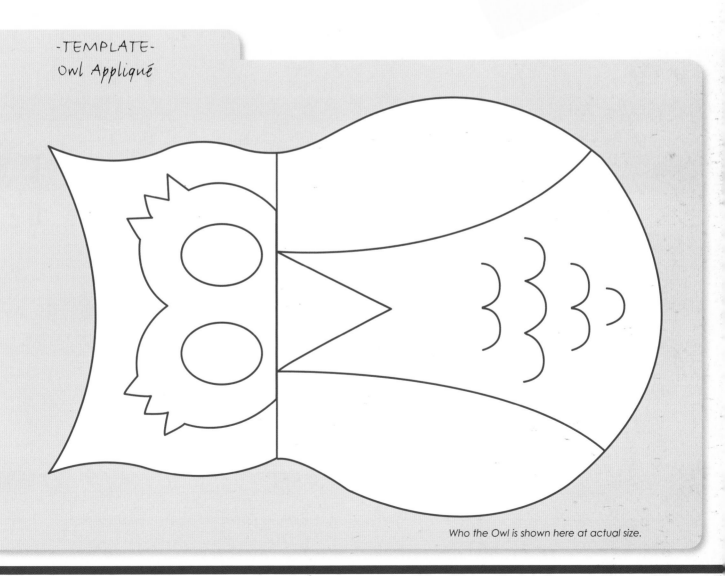

Who the Owl is shown here at actual size.

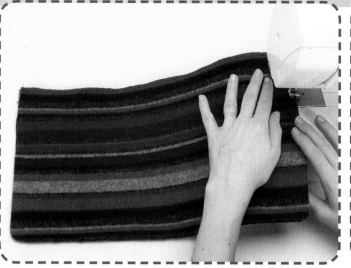

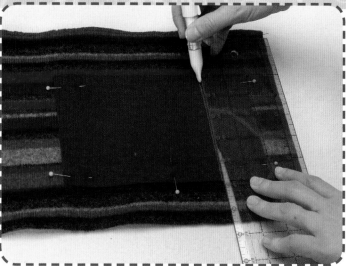

1. Prepare apron pieces, fuse together and stitch

Cut a piece of sweater felt and a coordinating piece of wool craft felt into two rectangles, each measuring 9" x 16" (23cm x 41cm). Using double-sided fusible web and with wrong sides facing, fuse the front and back of the apron together. Round the bottom right and left corners with scissors. Edge stitch around the entire perimeter of the apron.

2. Pin on pocket and mark placement for smaller pocket

Cut a 5" x 8" (13cm x 20cm) rectangle for the large pocket out of wool craft felt. Round the bottom right and left corners with scissors. Pin the pocket in place, approximately 1½" (4cm) from the bottom edge and 1½" (4cm) in from the right edge. Draw a line with a chalk liner or a disappearing-ink marker to mark the stitch line for a smaller pocket. The pocket on the apron as shown is a pencil pocket and is 2" (5cm) wide. Edge stitch the sides and bottom of the large pocket and the stitch line for the pencil pocket.

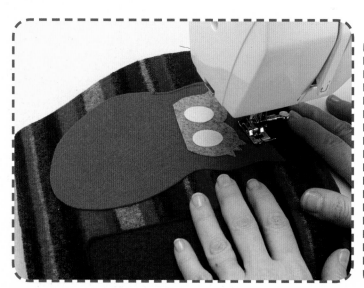

3. Fuse owl body, face and eyes to apron front

Use the patterns on page 87 to trace the owl's body, face, eyes and beak onto double-sided fusible web. Fuse the web to gray craft felt. (To customize for your scissors, trace inside finger holes to make eye shapes. This pattern fits 5" [13cm] Gingher embroidery sharps.) Cut out the owl's body, face and eyes, then fuse them to the apron. Edge stitch around the owl. See Techniques to Learn, pages 14–15, for instructions on fusing and appliqué.

4. Add beak and stitch feather details on owl's body

Using the pattern on page 87, cut out the owl pocket motifs from wool craft felt. Back the pocket with fusible interfacing for reinforcement. Fuse the wings and the beak to the pocket front using fusible web. Mark feather lines with a disappearing-ink marker, and then backstitch along the lines with embroidery floss. (See Techniques to Learn, page 12, for instructions on backstitch.) Machine stitch along the top pocket edge and around the beak.

5. Sew on owl pocket

Pin the pocket on top of the body shape on the apron. Edge stitch around the pocket sides and bottom. Then stitch down each of the inside wing lines.

6. Stitch on buttons and face details

Stitch on two buttons for the owl's eyes using embroidery floss or thread to match the buttons. Stitch around the perimeter of the owl's face with a contrasting color.

7. Attach ties

Cut two strips of wool 26" (66cm) long and 1" (3cm) wide for the apron's ties. Pin about 1" (3cm) of one tie to the top corner of the apron front and box stitch it into place. (Stitch a small box, and then stitch an X through the middle of the box for reinforcement.) Repeat for the other tie.

rainbow bag

materials

- felted sweaters
- cotton print fabric for lining
- rigid purse handles
- wool strips or twill tape
- sewing machine
- needle and thread
- scissors
- disappearing-ink marker or chalk liner
- straight pins

The sky's the limit with the multi-hued *Rainbow Bag*. A full spectrum of color adorns this simply constructed bag. Waves of scalloped felt layer to add pattern and texture to a basic foundation. Fun plastic handles and coordinated print lining of your choice are just the right details to make this bag complete. It's the perfect size for a quick trip out or an afternoon of shopping with your girlfriends.

Of course, your bag doesn't have to reflect the colors of the rainbow. Let your own scrap stash (or the weather!) inspire your color scheme: cool blues with grays (partly cloudy), reds with fuchsia (dramatic sunset) or charcoal with black (dark and stormy).

 BRIGHT IDEA

To expedite the process and allow yourself to play around with color placement before you begin, you may want to begin by cutting strips 2" (5cm) wide and at least 9½" (24cm) long. Cutting straight strips is easier and quicker than cutting waves, especially if you're using a rotary cutter and mat. Then play around and lay out the strips in the order you would like them to go before cutting them into waves.

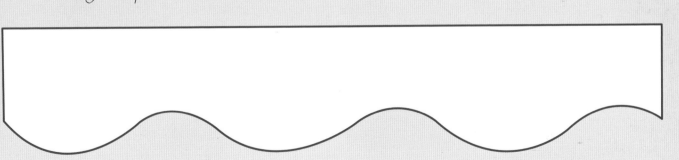

-TEMPLATE-
Wavy Strips

Enlarge template for wavy strips by 133% to bring to full size.

1. Cut wavy strips and begin to sew

Cut two 11" high x 10" wide (28cm x 54cm) rectangles out of felted sweaters for the front and back of the bag. Use the wavy template on page 91 to cut out sixteen strips of felted sweaters in various colors. Pin the bottom strip across the front about 2½" (6cm) up from the bottom of the bag. Straight stitch across the top of the strip, ⅛" (3mm) from the top of the strip, leaving a ¼" (6mm) space at either side of the bag front. See Techniques to Learn, page 12, for instructions on straight stitch.

2. Continue to sew on wavy strips

Flip the next strip so the waves alternate between the waves in the first strip. Pin the second strip about 1¼" (3cm) above the first strip (measuring from top edge to top edge). Straight stitch across the top of the second strip, again ⅛" (3mm) from the top edge of the strip, leaving a ¼" (6mm) space at either side of the bag front. Continue to sew on strips, using eight strips total, and leaving about ¾" (2cm) space above the final strip. Repeat for the back of the bag.

tip

Use a zipper foot for the side seams because the pieces are so thick and the seam allowance (¼" [6mm]) is relatively small.

3. Pin and sew back and front of bag together

With right sides together, pin the front and the back of the bag together along the sides and bottom, leaving the top open. Stitch the two sides together with ¼" (6mm) seam allowances, taking care not to catch any of the strips in the seam. Use the zipper foot if necessary (see tip on this page).

4. Pin, mark and stitch box bottom

Flatten one of the bottom corners of the bag, aligning the bottom and side seam, and pin it flat. Use a disappearing-ink marker or chalk liner to draw a line at a right angle to the seam 1" (3cm) from the corner of the bag. Stitch along the line to create a box corner. Repeat for the remaining bottom corner of the bag.

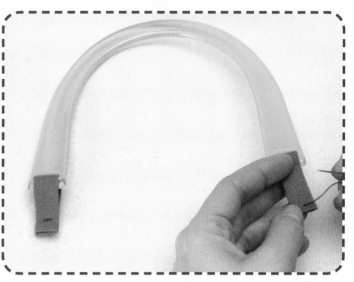

5. Sew lining

For the lining, cut two 11½" high x 10" wide (29cm x 25cm) rectangles out of a complementary fabric or fabrics. Pin the rectangles with right sides together. Stitch sides and bottom together with ¼" (6mm) seam allowances. Create box corners by stitching across the seams 1" (3cm) from the corner in the same manner as for the outer purse. If you're using a cotton print fabric for the lining, pink the seam allowance to prevent the edges from unraveling.

6. Tack wool tabs through handles

Cut four ½" x 3" (1cm x 8cm) tabs out of sturdy wool fabric (or use twill tape). Thread each tab through one of the handle slots and tack the ends of the tabs together.

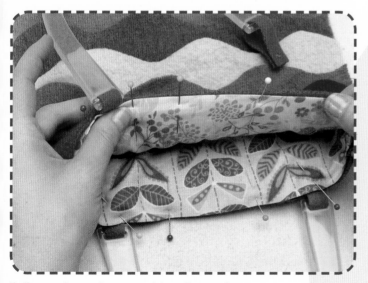

7. Pin and sew lining and handles to bag

Fold over and press the top of the lining about ¼" (6mm). Insert the lining into the bag with wrong sides facing, and mark the handle placement. Pin the top of the lining to the top of the bag, sandwiching the handle tabs between the lining and the bag. Straight stitch two rows around the top of the bag.

the cherry on top

The Cherry on Top is all about the extras...the finishing touches that complete the look. Maybe it's because accessories communicate our personal style to the rest of the world.

In this chapter, the accessories (the "cherries on top") are inspired by the vibrant colors and versatile nature of wool. Soft and tactile, felted wool that spent its former life as a sweater is given a new lease when transformed into a brilliant scarf (see the *Shibori Scarf* on page 110 or the *Boyfriend Scarf* on page 112) or a chic new bag or tote.

Watch the possibilities unfold! Whether you upgrade that humdrum cardigan with a colorful brooch (see page 104) or top off your outfit with the perfect hat (see the *Pillbox Hat* on page 96 or the *Bomber Hat* on page 122), you're sure to find a project that has you written all over it.

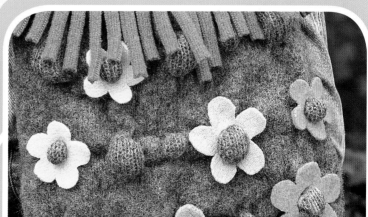

pillbox hat

The *Pillbox Hat* is a great topper to get you through a blustery day (or a bad hair day!) with style. Designed with simplicity in mind, it's a blank canvas to which you can add your own artistic flair. You can make it clean and modern or jazz it up with decorative details such as felt cutouts or reverse appliqué.

Just one simple measurement enables you to make the fit just right for anyone's noggin. So easy and quick, you'll want one to go with every coat you own.

materials

- felted sweaters
- wool craft felt
- yarn
- sewing machine
- iron and press cloth
- tailor's ham (optional)
- tapestry needle
- scissors
- straight pins
- measuring tape
- your head

BRIGHT IDEAS

* Use the circle on the top of the crown as a place for embellishment. Whipstitch an I-cord circle in a spiral pattern or appliqué a field of flowers.
* Experiment with shaping the rectangular cuff. Instead of hemming the edge, try cutting it in a decorative pattern such as scallops, waves or free-form jagged points.

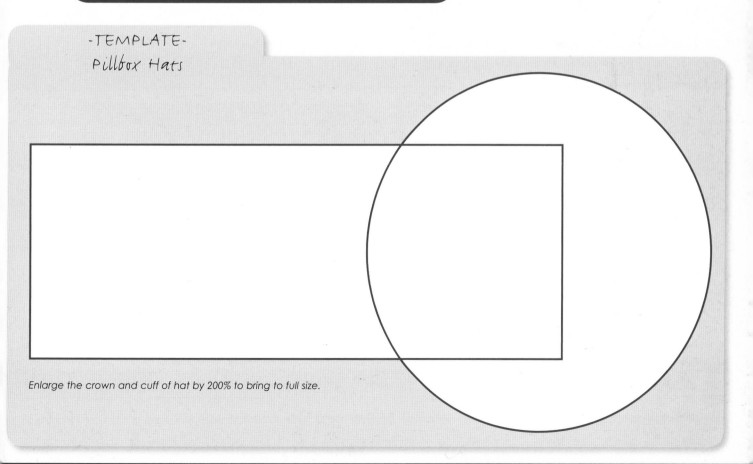

-TEMPLATE-
Pillbox Hats

Enlarge the crown and cuff of hat by 200% to bring to full size.

1. Sew crown and cuff

Cut out two sets of two 4½" x 11½" (11cm x 29cm) rectangles from felted sweaters for the sides of the hat. (See the tip below on sewing a hat with a perfect fit by adjusting the size of the rectangles.) With right sides together, pin and sew together the short ends of each set of rectangles, leaving a ¼" (6mm) seam allowance. (See Techniques to Learn, page 12, for information on straight stitch.) Press the seam allowances open on the wrong side with a steam iron. One of these sets will be the crown of the hat, and the other set will be the cuff.

2. Pin and sew top of hat to crown

Cut one 7½" (19cm) diameter circle out of sweater felt for the top of the hat. With right sides together, pin the edge of the crown around the hat top, distributing the fabric evenly. Sew with a ¼" (6mm) seam allowance. Press the seam allowance open on the wrong side with a steam iron.

tip

To make a hat with a perfect fit, measure around the head of the person you are making the hat for. Wrap a thin, rigid tape measure around the widest part of the head. Continue to hold the tape measure in a circle as you remove it from the head. Use the tape measure circle as a template to trace the hat top. To find the length of the cuff and crown rectangles, divide the head measurement by two and add ½" (1cm) for seam allowances.

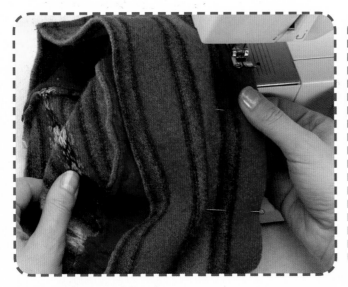

3. Pin and sew cuff to hat

Align the right side of the cuff to the wrong side of the crown. Align the side seams of the cuff and crown, and pin them together. Sew the pieces together, leaving a ¼" (6mm) seam allowance.

4. Add flower embellishments

To hem the cuff edge, fold over ½" (1cm) of fabric, pin and straight stitch the edge, being careful not to stretch the fabric while sewing. Turn the entire hat right-side out and fold up the cuff. Cover the hat with a press cloth and steam it over a tailor's ham (or use a rolled-up towel). To embellish the cuff, cut out felt flowers and stitch an X in the center of each one with coordinating yarn.

Reverse Appliqué Hat

For a variation on the *Pillbox Hat*, try a bit of reverse appliqué on the cuff for an added graphic pop of color. It's easiest to do this before assembling the hat.

1. Sew on appliqué

Cut out circles of wool craft felt in several colors to embellish the cuff with reverse appliqué. Place the circles on the wrong side of the cuff pieces, keeping all circles ½" (1cm) away from the edges of the cuff. Straight stitch around the perimeter of each circle, ⅛" (3mm) from the edge of the felt circle, using thread to match the cuff color.

2. Cut away fabric at back of appliqué

Turn the cuff over, and use sharp pointed scissors to trim away the cuff fabric inside the stitching line to reveal the appliqué.

To evenly distribute the fabric when attaching the crown to the top of the hat, mark the four compass points by folding the hat top and marking the fold at the edge of the circle, and then folding the circle again in the opposite direction and marking again. Pin the top of the hat to the crown at these four marks, aligning with the side seams, center back and center front. Pin the fabric evenly between the four pins.

tip

3. Stitch around appliqué

Stitch with yarn, using a running stitch, around each circle on the right side of the cuff. (See Techniques to Learn, page 13, for instructions on working in running stitch.) Finish the hat in the same way as for the hat shown on page 98.

peas and carrots purse

materials

unfelted feltable sweater
felted sweater with ribbing
2 rigid purse handles
½ yd (46cm) cotton print fabric for lining
approx 20 large beads, small Styrofoam balls, etc.
approx 20 small rubber bands
needle and thread
sewing machine
iron and press cloth
straight pins
scissors

I love the rich, textured look of a cable-knit or crocheted purse. I wanted to create a similar appearance with felting. The shibori technique (see the *Shibori Scarf* on page 110) is just the ticket for adding surface dimension. The *Peas and Carrots Purse* offers just that: green bauble "peas" dot the bag, and orange "carrot stick" fringe dangles from the handles. For extra detail, cut out flower shapes to pop onto the baubles. If you're not one for veggies, play with another color scheme.

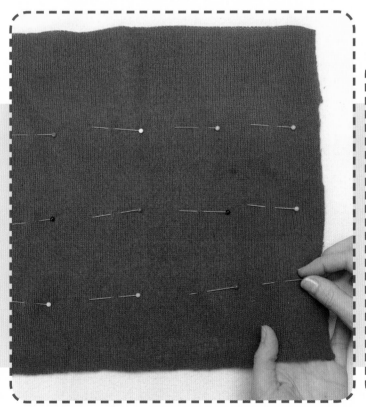

1. Mark placement for balls

Remove the sleeves and ribbing from an unfelted sweater and steam it flat from the wrong side. The piece should measure about 12" (30cm) wide by 14" (36cm) high. Use straight pins to mark the position of the large and small balls. Space the pins about 2" to 3" (5cm to 8cm) apart. Place pins for three rows of balls (twelve total).

2. Rubber-band balls in place

Place a ball under a pin from the back of the sweater. Remove the pin and wrap a rubber band around the ball from the front of sweater. Wrap the band around repeatedly until it's snug. Continue until ten large balls and ten small balls are secured. Duplicate the ball pattern for the back of the purse.

3. Felt bag front and back, remove beads

Place the front and back of the bag into a lingerie bag. Felt the pieces in the washing machine. After the first cycle, check to see if the desired felting has been achieved. If not, run it through the washer again. Put the pieces in the dryer on low, then air dry. Once they're completely dry, remove the rubber bands and beads. Press the "non-shiboried" edges of the fabric from the wrong side with a steam iron.

4. Trim front and back of bag to proper size

Without stretching the fabric, cut both the front and back of the bag into into a rectangle measuring about 12" (30cm) long by 10½" (27cm) wide. Don't worry if your pieces are a bit "wobbly." That's the nature of shibori!

5. Seam purse front and back together

With right sides together, pin the front and back of the purse together. Sew the pieces together, leaving 3" (8cm) open below the top edge (to allow for vents at purse opening).

6. Sew box bottom corners

Flatten the bottom corner (side seam to bottom seam) and pin it in place. Stitch across each corner, 1" (3cm) from the point. Trim the excess fabric about ¼" (6mm) from the stitch line. Repeat for the other bottom corner.

7. Sew lining and steam vents

Cut two 12" x 10½" (30cm x 27cm) rectangles for the lining (or same measurement as outer bag). Fold the top edge down ¼" (6mm) toward the wrong side and edge stitch to create a finished edge. With right sides together, sew the front and back together, starting and stopping 3" (8cm) below the top edge (for vents). Sew box bottom corners as for the outer part of the bag. Press the vent seam allowances back at the top 3" (8cm) of the lining.

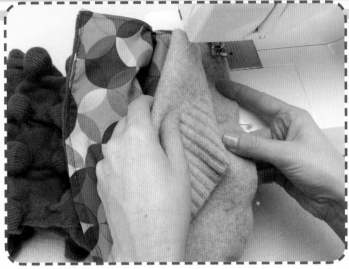

8. Pin lining in place

With wrong sides together, place the lining inside the outer bag. Pin the lining and the outside of the bag together along the top edge and along the side vents. Edge stitch the lining to the outer bag around the top edges and side vents.

9. Sew first part of casing to top of bag

Cut two 5" x 10" (13cm x 25cm) rectangles out of a felted sweater in a contrast color for the handle casings. Utilize the ribbed edge of the sweater. The ribbing should be about 2" to 3" (5cm to 8cm) to cut for fringe in addition to the 5" (13cm) measurement. Pin the right side of the casing to the lining side of the top edge of the bag. Ease in fullness of outer bag and pin all three layers together, then edge stitch.

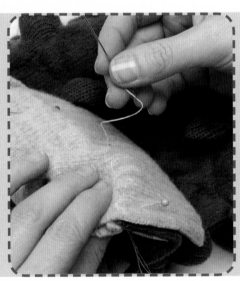

10. Hand baste casing to outer part of bag

Flip the casing to the outside of the bag. Put the casing through one of the wooden handles. Hand baste the top edge of the ribbing to the first casing seam. Machine stitch on top of the basting stitch, keeping the handle clear of the needle. (Use a zipper foot, if necessary.) Repeat steps 9 and 10 to sew the casing on the other side of the bag.

11. Cut fringe

Cut between the ribs on the casing to create fringe.

12. Add flower embellishment

For added embellishment, hand-cut flower shapes using the pattern on page 127 from various felted sweater scraps and place them over the shibori baubles. Tack the flowers down with thread.

brooches

Brooches have certainly made a comeback in the last few years. And why not? Brooches are the quickest way to brighten up any part of your wardrobe. Add an instant accent to your hat, jacket or bag. Each design has its own possibilities for creative evolution. Consider combining the felt with other fabrics such as vintage prints or velvet. Try substituting beads in place of felt balls. Get out your stash of trimmings, buttons and doodads, and get started!

materials

felted sweater scraps
wool craft felt
cotton print fabric
double-sided fusible web
felted I-cord
wool yarn
felt balls
beads
button
embroidery floss
decorative beading wire
1¼" (3cm) pin backs
disappearing-ink marker
tapestry needle
sewing needle and thread

needle-felting tools
Fray Check (optional)
fabric glue
iron and press cloth
scissors
straightedge

Sprouts Brooch

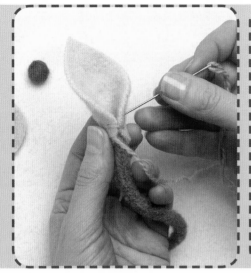

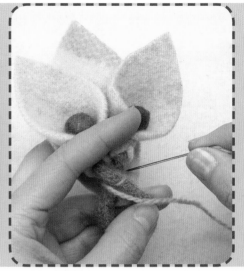

1. Secure petal to stem

Use the templates on page 141 to cut out one leaf and two petal shapes from felted sweater scraps. Cut 5" (13cm) of felted I-cord in a contrasting color. Wrap one petal piece around one end of the I-cord. Use yarn and a tapestry needle to stitch an X through the petal and I-cord to secure them together.

2. Stitch on felt ball

Without cutting your yarn, bring the needle up through the center of the flower and thread the needle through a felt ball. If desired, you may add a decorative French knot at the top of the felt ball. Repeat steps 1 and 2 to secure a petal and felt ball to the other end of the I-cord stem.

3. Sew over I-cord stem

Place the petals on top of the leaf shape and stitch the petals to the leaf, hiding the yarn behind the I-cord. Allow the I-cord to twist, and add a decorative stitch with yarn at the overlap to secure the shape.

5. Glue on pin back

Apply fabric glue to the back of the pin and apply it to the back of the leaf, covering any threads.

4. Cut slits for pin back

Using the template on page 141, cut a piece of felt for the pin back. Pierce the felt piece in two places to accommodate the pin, and push the latch and the pin through the slits.

BRIGHT IDEA

Go for a stroll in your garden or visit the local flower shop for some botanical inspiration. Bring a digital camera and take pictures of different varieties and color combinations. Use these for reference when you are making your brooches. Imagine the beautiful work of Georgia O'Keeffe!

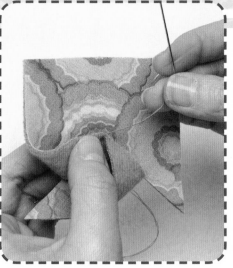

1. Mark X on fused square

Draw a 3" (8cm) square onto the paper backing of a sheet of fusible web. Fuse the web to a piece of cotton print fabric on the bias. Cut out the print square and fuse it to the back of a felted sweater scrap. (See Techniques to Learn, page 14, for instructions on fusing.) Cut out the fused square. Use a straightedge and a disappearing-ink marker to make an X from corner to corner.

2. Cut square to create pinwheel effect

Cut along each X line for 1" (3cm), beginning at the corner and cutting in toward the center.

3. Fold and tack pinwheel petals

Fold every other point in toward the center, creating a pinwheel effect. Tack the points down in the center with thread.

tip

Use Fray Check on the cut edges of the print fabric to keep them from fraying.

4. Cut out flower center

Use the template on page 141 to cut out a small circle from a piece of wool craft felt for the center of the flower. Trim out four small wedges at 12, 3, 6 and 9 o'clock, then cut out more wedges between the first wedges.

5. Stitch brooch layers together

Use the pattern on page 141 to cut out a four-point star shape onto another color of felted sweater scrap. Cut out the shape. Layer the star, pinwheel and flower center together. Hold a button in place on the top, and stitch through the button and all the layers to secure them together. Create a pin back for the pinwheel as for the *Sprouts Brooch* (see page 105, Steps 4 and 5).

Butterfly Brooch

1. Cut out butterfly and add needle-felting detail

Use the template on page 141 to trace a butterfly shape onto a scrap of felted sweater. Cut out the butterfly. Freehand the wing detail with a disappeaing-ink pen or a chalk liner and needle felt the yarn along those lines. Steam press the butterfly from the back to set the yarn.

2. Fuse decorative backing to butterfly

Trace the butterfly shape onto the paper backing of a piece of fusible web. Fuse the web to a piece of cotton print fabric. Cut out the butterfly, and remove the paper and fuse it to the back of the felt butterfly. Trim along the edges to clean up the butterfly.

3. Blanket stitch around butterfly

With a complementary shade of embroidery floss, blanket stitch around the edge of the butterfly. See Techniques to Learn, page 13, for instructions on blanket stitch.

tip *If you have wimpy fingers, use pliers to hold one end of the wires as you twist the antennae.*

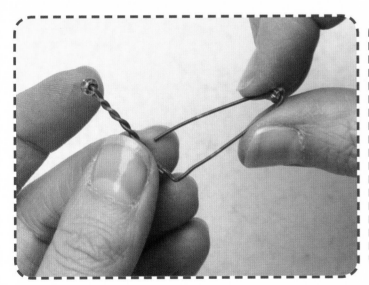

4. Twist antenna

For the antennae, cut about 4" (10cm) of colored wire. Thread one bead onto the wire, about 1" (3cm) from one end. Fold the wire back and twist it together. Repeat with another bead 1" (3cm) down from the other end of the wire. Hand-sew the wire antennae to the top center front of the butterfly.

5. Sew on butterfly body

Hand-sew felt balls up the center of the butterfly to make the body, hiding the antennae attachment with the top felt ball. If desired, hand-sew beads to the wings as a final touch. Use the template on page 141 to create a pin back for the butterfly, cutting and adjusting the back as for the *Sprouts Brooch* (see page 105, Steps 4 and 5).

mixed messenger bag

Soft yet structured, the *Mixed Messenger Bag* combines form and function. Just the right size for whatever your day may have in store: a guidebook, metro map and a croissant (or a board book, baby wipes and some Cheerios!). Made from bulkier sweaters for stability, the seam allowances are kept to the outside of the bag for a more casual, less constructed look. Explore various color schemes or try different trimming details along the flap edge such as pompoms, I-cord or fringe.

materials

2 13" wide x 11" high (33cm x 28cm) pieces of felted sweaters for front and back of bag

12½" wide x 11" high (32cm x 28cm) piece of felted sweater for flap

wool craft felt

double-sided fusible web

felt balls

sewing machine

scissors

straight pins

straightedge

BRIGHT IDEA

If you've felted a sweater "too far" and end up with a very thick material, the Mixed Messenger Bag is just the project to make lemonade out of that lemon. Felt that is too heavy for clothing is just right for this bag.

1. Sew slip pocket to back of bag

Cut a 6½" x 7½" (17cm x 19cm) rectangle out of a felted sweater scrap for the back slip pocket, utilizing ribbing for the top. Center the slip pocket on the back panel 2½" (6cm) from the top edge. Edge stitch the sides and bottom of the pocket to the back panel, backstitching at the top edge of the pocket to reinforce it.

2. Fuse and edge stitch strap

Cut a 2" x 38" (5cm x 97cm) piece of felted sweater for the strap (or cut to desired length). Cut a strap lining of the same dimensions out of wool craft felt. (If you don't have a sweater and/or a piece of craft felt long enough to accommodate the dimensions of the strap, piece several rectangles together with zigzag seaming.) Fuse the strap and lining together with double-sided fusible web. (See Techniques to Learn, page 14, for instructions on fusing.) Edge stitch all the way around the sides and ends of the strap.

3. Seam strap to sides of bag

Sew the right side of the strap to the wrong side of the side panel, overlapping 1¼" (3cm). Stitch a 1" x 2" (3cm x 5cm) box with an X through the middle for reinforcement. Repeat for the other side panel.

4. Pin sides to bottom of bag

With wrong sides together, pin the ends of the side panels to the bottom panel of the bag, keeping the seam allowances on the outside of the bag. Sew the side and bottom pieces together, keeping seam allowances to the outside.

5. Assemble bag

With wrong sides together, pin the back panel to the sides and bottom of the bag. Stitch the pieces together, keeping the seam allowances facing outward. Stitch directly up to each corner and stop. Now sew into the corner from the other direction. Sewing seams this way is easier than stitching over the thick corner seam allowances. Repeat for the front panel.

6. Sew on flap

Lap the top edge of the front flap over the top edge of the back panel, leaving a ¼" (6mm) space on either side. Stitch the flap to the front of the bag with a lapped seam. Hand-stitch a 1" (3cm) hem on the front flap. Hand-sew felt balls along the folded edge.

shibori scarf

unfelted feltable
wool sweater (XL)

approx 40 large beads,
small Styrofoam balls, etc.
in various sizes

approx 40 small rubber bands

straight pins

disappearing-ink
marker or chalk liner

sewing machine

iron and press cloth

No Fray (optional)

scissors

I first learned about shibori felting from a workshop at my local yarn shop, and I've been intrigued by it ever since! Shibori is a term for a traditional Japanese tie-dye technique. Apply it to felting (minus the dye) and amazing dimensional textures result! Sections of fabric are manipulated through stitching and tying before felting. Wrap unfelted fabric around differently shaped objects (think beads, corks, bottle caps, etc.) to produce varying textures. During felting, these objects resist while the surrounding fabric felts and shrinks, producing marvelous tactile results. The *Shibori Scarf* is a fun way to play with this surface-altering technique.

tip

Before starting the project, cut one sleeve off the sweater and felt it in the washing machine. If the sleeve felts sufficiently, proceed with the project. If not, try with another sweater. This will save you the time of rubber-banding all the beads to then discover that the material doesn't felt. To increase the durability of the scarf, add No Fray to the edges of cut circles.

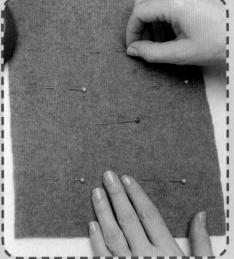

1. Stitch rectangles together

Remove the ribbing from an unfelted sweater and steam it flat from the wrong side. Cut the sweater into four rectangles, each about 7" (18cm) wide and as long as possible. The total length of the combined rectangles should be about 70" to 80" (178cm to 203cm). Straight stitch the short ends of the rectangles to one another to create the scarf. See Techniques to Learn, page 12, for instructions on straight stitch.

2. Mark positions for beads

Starting with one end of the scarf, mark with pins the positions you want the largest beads to have. The pins should be about 2½" to 3" (6cm to 8cm) apart.

3. Rubber-band beads in place

Place a bead under the scarf and line it up with a pin. Remove the pin and wrap the rubber band around the bead from the front of the scarf. Wrap the band around repeatedly until it's snug. Continue until about six large beads are secured. Using smaller beads, fill in the spaces between the first beads, securing each one with a rubber band. Repeat for the other end of the scarf.

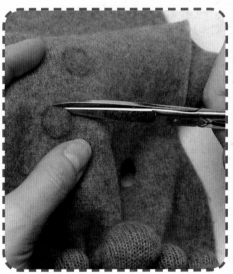

4. Felt scarf and remove beads

Place the scarf into a lingerie bag. Follow the felting techniques in the washing machine. After the first cycle, check the scarf to see if desired felting has been achieved. If not, run it through again. Dry it in the dryer on low, then air dry. Once it's completely dry, remove the rubber bands and beads.

5. Trim edges of scarf

Press the "non-shiboried" part of the scarf from the wrong side with a steam iron. Mark a wavy or scalloped edge with disappearing-ink marker or chalk liner. Cut along the line with scissors.

6. Cut away dots to make circles

Mark random dots with disappearing-ink marker or chalk liner. Cut them out with scissors.

boyfriend scarf

Materials

**felted sweater scraps
rotary cutter and mat
sewing machine
straightedge**

Sometimes it's hard to make something for the men in our lives, especially something wearable. There can be a fine line between making a stylish statement and making a spectacle of him! Keeping that in mind, stripes can be a subtle way to add color and pattern to a guy's wardrobe. The *Boyfriend Scarf* uses straightforward strips of color put together in a brick-and-mortar fashion. The scarf ends in an uneven design for a slightly offbeat finish.

BRIGHT IDEA

Don't let the name of this scarf hold you back. Different color schemes can change the attitude of this design dramatically. Try pink and brown for your best friend or brights for the kids.

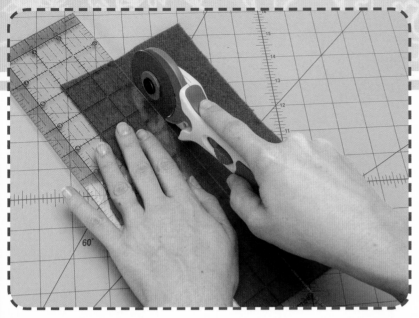

1. Cut strips

Use a rotary cutter to cut 2" (5cm) strips of felted sweater scraps in varying lengths (about 4" to 12" [10cm x 30cm] long).

2. Arrange strips and seam together

Alternating color/pattern, lay out your strips, end to end, in three long rows. Each row should be the same length, the finished scarf length desired. Working with one row at a time, sew the strips together with zigzag stitch, butting the ends together. See Techniques to Learn, page 12, for instructions on zigzag stitch.

3. Stagger edges of sewn strips and stitch together

After all three rows are sewn, lay them out side by side. Offset the ends of each row to create a "stepped" end. Zigzag stitch two rows together. Zigzag stitch the third row to the first two rows.

BRIGHT IDEA

For a little holiday elfin magic, add length to the fingertip area of the mitten pattern and shape it into a point. Sew on a pompom at the tip or a bell for Christmas mittens.

cozy mittens

We never outgrow mittens, do we? This project is an excellent scrap-user-upper and a great opportunity for experimentation. Put together scraps and colors you might not normally use together. Perhaps make the left and right mitten different from one another. Needle felt your favorite flower or motif, or use the design provided.

Any way you make them, these mittens are a wonderful way to keep warm, be original and add a little sunshine to your day.

materials

- felted sweater scraps
- wool craft felt
- yarn
- embroidery floss
- sewing machine
- iron and press cloth
- needle-felting tools
- tapestry needle
- scissors
- straight pins

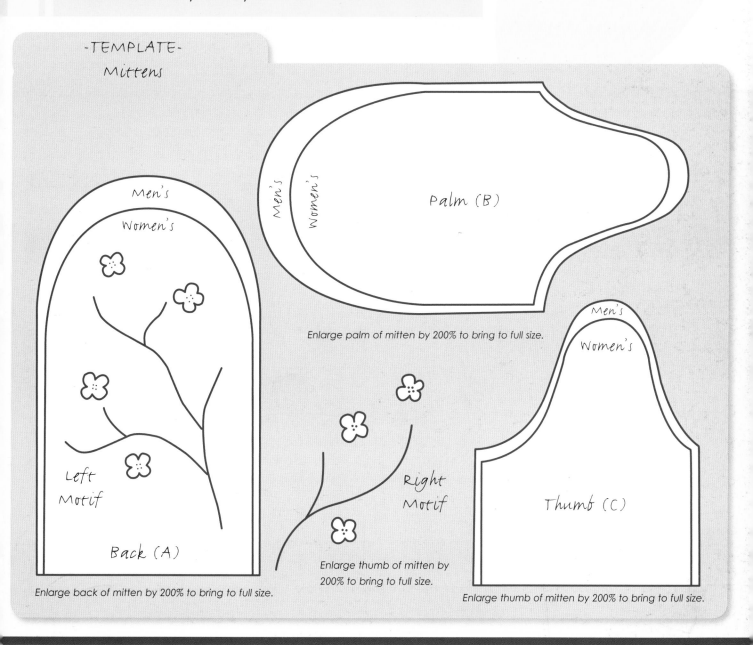

-TEMPLATE-
Mittens

Men's
Women's

Left
Motif

Back (A)

Enlarge back of mitten by 200% to bring to full size.

Men's
Women's

Palm (B)

Enlarge palm of mitten by 200% to bring to full size.

Right
Motif

Enlarge thumb of mitten by 200% to bring to full size.

Men's
Women's

Thumb (C)

Enlarge thumb of mitten by 200% to bring to full size.

1. Cut mitten pieces and lay out

Use the pattern provided on page 115 to cut out two of each pattern piece. You'll have two back pieces (A), two palm pieces (B) and two thumb pieces (C). For one set of pieces, reverse the palm and thumb (B and C) to create a left-hand mitten. Cut two pieces of felted sweater ribbing for the cuffs. For women's mittens, the ribbed pieces should measure 7½" (19cm) x 3½" (9cm). For men's mittens, the ribbed pieces should measure 8½" (22cm) x 3½" (9cm).

2. Sew thumb to palm

With right sides together, sew the mitten thumb (B) to the thumb part of the mitten palm (C), leaving ¼" (6mm) seam allowances. See Techniques to Learn, page 12, for instructions on straight stitch.

3. Pin and sew mitten front and back together

With right sides together, pin and sew the palm and thumb piece (B/C) to the back (A) of the mitten. Trim seam allowances to ⅛" (3mm), and turn the mitten right-side out. Steam press the mitten using a press cloth.

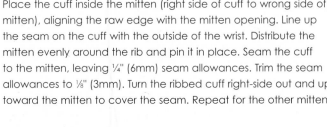

5. Pin and sew cuff to mitten

Place the cuff inside the mitten (right side of cuff to wrong side of mitten), aligning the raw edge with the mitten opening. Line up the seam on the cuff with the outside of the wrist. Distribute the mitten evenly around the rib and pin it in place. Seam the cuff to the mitten, leaving ¼" (6mm) seam allowances. Trim the seam allowances to ⅛" (3mm). Turn the ribbed cuff right-side out and up toward the mitten to cover the seam. Repeat for the other mitten.

4. Sew mitten cuffs

Fold the ribbing lengthwise. With right sides together, sew the ends of the cuff together. Turn the cuff right-side out.

Needle-Felted Mittens

To accent solid-color sweater felt, add some needle-felted details before constructing the mittens.

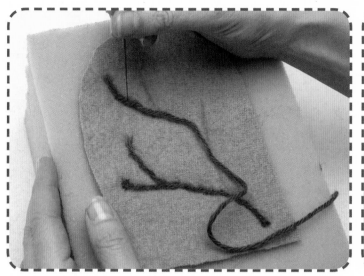

1. Draw design and needle felt

Use a disappearing-ink marker or a chalk liner to draw your design onto the front of the mitten. Trace the design provided (see page 115) or make your own. Place the mitten front on top of the foam mat. Lay yarn along the stems and needle felt them into place with a felting needle.

2. Sew on flowers

Using the templates on page 115, cut out several felt flowers and stitch them into place with French knots (see page 12) around the branches.

Manly Mittens

These mittens are really just a larger version of the women's mittens. Choose "manly" colors and stripes for a more masculine mitten.

just right tote

Most felted totes come from the school of "knit first, then felt"—but unpredictable shrinking and skewing during the felting process can leave you with a surprise on your hands. If you're hesitant about your tote turning out just the right size, you'll like my "felt first, then sew" philosophy. Cut from large prefelted sweater pieces, the *Just Right Tote* can be whatever you need it to be. Follow the dimensions provided for a handy "everyday"-sized tote, or alter them to fit your own desires. The clean, uncluttered design affords plenty of space for extra pockets or embellishment.

- felted sweater
- ½ yd (46cm) wool craft felt
- purchased tote handles
- double-sided fusible web
- sewing machine
- iron and press cloth
- scissors
- straight pins

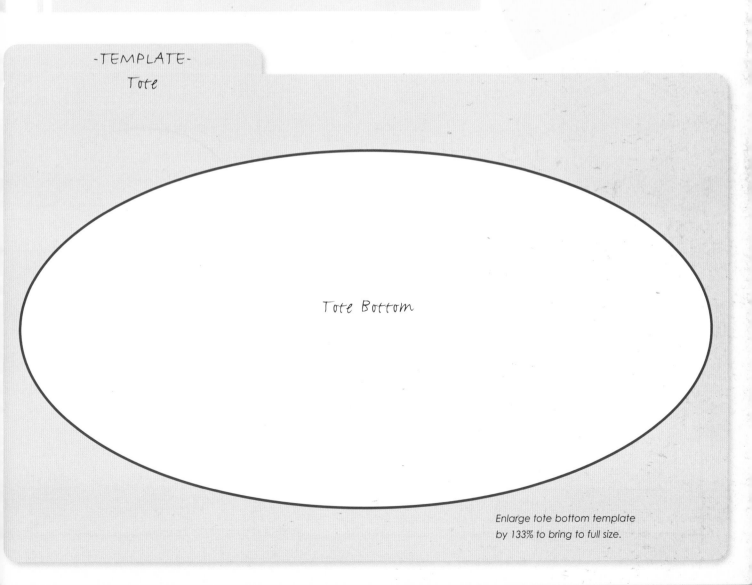

-TEMPLATE-
Tote

Tote Bottom

Enlarge tote bottom template by 133% to bring to full size.

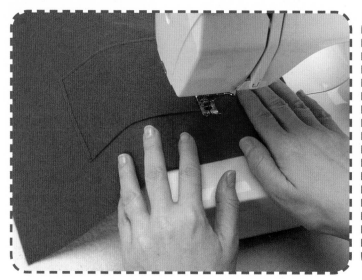

1. Stitch inside pocket

Center a 4" x 5" (10cm x 13cm) felt rectangle on one of the 12" x 12" (30cm x 30cm) felt lining squares, about 2" (5cm) below the top edge. (This piece will be the lining for the back panel.) Edge stitch around the pocket to secure it to the lining. Backstitch both top corners of the pocket to reinforce the top edge of the pocket opening.

2. Fuse tote pieces together

Apply fusible web to the back of each 12" x 12" (30cm x 30cm) lining square. Cut one oval of felt for the tote bottom, following the pattern on page 119, and apply fusible web to the back of the oval. Remove the paper backing and fuse the pieces to felted sweater pieces (two more squares the same size as the lining and one oval for the outside of the bag bottom). Thoroughly steam press from the wool felt side to ensure fusion. Trim away any excess. See Techniques to Learn, page 14, for instructions on fusing.

If you'd like to give your tote a little something extra, you can make a simple brooch and attach it to the bag as a special embellishment, as I did with the version shown on page 118. See the instructions for the Butterfly Brooch on page 107 to make one of your own.

3. Stitch outside pocket onto front of bag

Cut a 5½" x 4½" (14cm x 11cm) piece of felted sweater for the outside pocket, utilizing a ribbed edge from the sweater scrap for the top edge of the pocket. Center the pocket on the front panel, 3" (8cm) below the top edge. Pin the pocket and edge stitch around it, reinforcing the top edges of the pocket opening as for the inside pocket.

4. Stitch tabs to handles

Cut four 1" x 3" (3cm x 8cm) felt tabs for securing the handles. Put each felt handle tab through one of the ring ends of the handles. Fold and stitch a 1" (3cm) square to secure the ends of the tabs together, using the zipper foot if needed. Repeat for the remaining three tabs and rings.

6. Sew side seams

With lining sides together, sew the side seams of the tote, leaving a ¼" (6mm) seam allowance. (The seam allowance is on the outside of the tote.) Backstitch the top and bottom edges for reinforcement.

5. Sew handles in place and edge stitch around top of bag front and back

Pin one set of handles to the lining side of the front panel 5½" (14cm) apart. Stitch the handle tabs to the tote, following the previously stitched square. Repeat to secure the handles to the back panel. Edge stitch the top edge of the front and back panels.

7. Pin and sew bag bottom

Fold the oval for the bag bottom in half lengthwise and place a pin at each halfway point as a guide for where to pin it to the sides of the bag. Pin the bottom oval to the side seams of the tote, lining sides together. Straight stitch the bottom to the sides, leaving a ¼" (6mm) seam allowance on the outside of the bag. When seaming the bottom, stitch to the corner, pick up the foot and cut the thread, then resume stitching directly after the corner. (It's easiest to stitch into the corner.)

bomber hat

This hat was inspired by so many others: a traditional Russian trooper mink hat, an aviator flight hat and (dare I say it) Elmer Fudd's hunting cap! The *Bomber Hat* is retro, yet modern in styling, and it's incredibly warm and versatile. Side flaps tie at the crown or flip down to cover your ears when it's really cold out (or to block out unwanted comments on the ski slope). It's fully lined, so choose lighter-weight felted sweaters in contrasting colors or patterns.

materials

felted sweaters in 2 colors: one for the outer color and one contrasting lining color

wool craft felt strips

sewing machine

needle and thread

iron and press cloth

tailor's ham (optional)

scissors

straight pins

Sizes

See the templates on page 142 for sizing information.

tip

After you've attached the lining, you'll need to snip the seam allowances on the curves. Snip tiny slits on the concave curves and notches on the convex curves. This will give the hat nice smooth lines when you turn it right-side out.

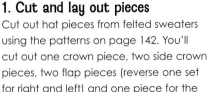

1. Cut and lay out pieces

Cut out hat pieces from felted sweaters using the patterns on page 142. You'll cut out one crown piece, two side crown pieces, two flap pieces (reverse one set for right and left) and one piece for the bill. Cut out a second set for the lining from a solid-color felted sweater.

2. Sew center lining to crown lining

Starting with the pieces for the hat's lining, pin and sew the crown sides with right sides together to the center crown panel, aligning center points and distributing evenly, leaving a ¼" (6mm) seam allowance. Steam press the seam allowances open from the wrong side using a tailor's ham (or use a rolled-up towel instead). See Techniques to Learn, page 12, for instructions on straight stitch.

3. Seam lining flaps together

With right sides together, sew the short edges of the earflap/cuff lining pieces together.

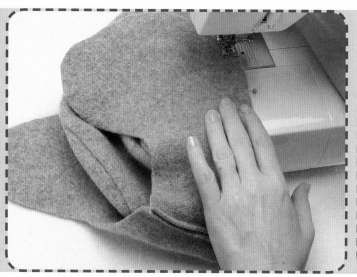 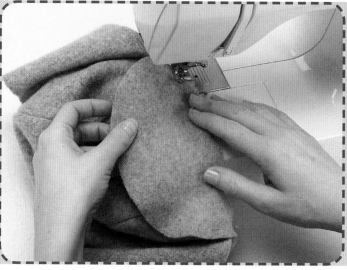

4. Pin and sew lining flaps to crown

Match up the center back of the earflap/cuff lining piece with the center back of the crown lining piece, and pin them together with right sides facing. Sew the earflap pieces to the crown.

5. Pin and sew bill lining to hat lining

Pin the bill lining piece to the center front crown of the lining with right sides together. Sew the bill lining to the crown.

6. Pin ties to lining

Cut two 8" (20cm) lengths of ⅜" (10mm) wide felt for the hat's ties. Pin each tie to each earflap lining at the center of each earflap as shown.

7. Pin lining into hat

Construct the outer part of the hat in the same way as the lining (see steps 1 through 5). With right sides together, pin the lining inside the outer part of the hat. Sew all the way around the lining, leaving a ¼" (6mm) seam allowance, and leaving the 3" (8cm) at the back cuff unsewn for turning. Clip notches in the seam allowances at the curves.

8. Press hat

Turn the entire hat right-side out through the 3" (8cm) opening, working out the curves with your fingers. Cover the hat with a press cloth, and steam the seams to shape the hat using a tailor's ham (or a rolled-up towel).

9. Hand-stitch opening closed

Hand-stitch the back opening closed, folding in the seam allowances of the lining and the outer fabric of the hat.

10. Edge stitch

For a clean, finished look, edge stitch around the entire perimeter of the hat where the lining meets the outer hat fabric. For a softer look, skip edge stitching.

11. Tack up bill

Tack up the bill in two places along the crown seams using a thread color to match the lining.

caring for your felted items

Lucky for you, felted wool has some wonderful natural properties that help keep it clean and dry. It is water resistant, stain resistant and even odor resistant. However, it can definitely still get dirty, especially if it's in constant use by a two-legged or four-legged little creature. When you need to clean a felted item, it's best to hand-wash it in cold water with a gentle soap. You may also machine wash a felted piece in a zippered pillowcase on the gentle cycle in cold water. Once the item is clean, lay it flat to dry.

resources

Most of the supplies used to make the projects in this book can be found in your local craft, hobby, bead or discount department stores. If you have trouble locating a specific product, contact one of the supply sources listed below to find a local or Internet vendor or to request a catalog. Shop at your local thrift shops or secondhand stores to find great feltable sweaters.

Craft Tools and Notions

Prym Consumer USA, Inc.
P.O. Box 5028
Spartanburg, SC 29304
www.dritz.com
sewing, quilting, cutting and craft-related tools and notions

Fiskars Brands, Inc.
2537 Daniels Street
Madison, WI 53718
866.348.5661
school, office and craft supplies
www.fiskars.com

Caron International, Inc.
P.O. Box 222
Washington, NC 27889
www.caron.com
Embellish Knit Cordmaker

Clover Needlecraft, Inc.
13438 Alondra Boulevard
Cerritos, CA 90703
800.233.1703
www.clover-usa.com
needle-felting tools

Ornamentea
Bedizen Ornaments
509 North West Street
Raleigh, NC 27603
919.834.6260
www.ornamentea.com
felt balls and wool roving

National Nonwovens
P.O. Box 150
Easthampton, MA 01027
800.333.3469
www.woolfelt.com
wool craft felt

Therm O Web
770 Glenn Avenue
Wheeling, IL 60090
847.520.5200
www.thermoweb.com
fusible webbing

The Warm Company
5529 186th Place SW
Lynnwood, WA 98037
425.248.2424
fusible webbing

Thrifted Sweaters

Goodwill Industries
www.goodwill.org

Savers
www.savers.com

patterns

Enlarge templates for Nest Family Album
(page 24) by 133% to bring to full size.

Album Front
Bottom

Album Front
Top

Flower
Center

Template for center of flower on
Scrapwork Pillow (page 28) shown at
actual size.

Flower

Template for flower on Scrapwork Pillow (page 28), for flower on
Christmas Stocking variation (page 37) and for flower on Peas and
Carrot Purse (page 100) shown at actual size.

Eggs

Enlarge template for eggs for the Breakfast-in-Bed Pillow
(page 30) by 133% to bring to full size.

Grapefruit

Template for grapefruit for the
Breakfast-in-Bed Pillow (page 30)
shown at actual size.

Toast

Butter Pat

Fork

Strawberry
Leaf

Template for strawberry
leaf for the Breakfast-
in-Bed Pillow (page 30)
shown at actual size.

Template for toast for the Breakfast-in-Bed Pillow
(page 30) shown at actual size.

Template for strawberry for the
Breakfast-in-Bed Pillow (page 30)
shown at actual size.

Strawberry

Template for fork for
the Breakfast-in-Bed
Pillow (page 30) shown
at actual size.

Bacon

Bacon
Templates for bacon for the Breakfast-in-Bed Pillow (page 30) shown at actual size.

stocking shaft

Enlarge template for the shaft of the Christmas Stocking (page 34) by 133% to bring to full size.

Rosette

Leaf

Template for the leaf of the Christmas Stocking variation (page 37) shown at actual size.

Enlarge template for the rosette of the Christmas Stocking variation (page 37) by 133% to bring to full size.

Yo-yo Circle

Enlarge template for the yo-yo circle used for the Christmas Stocking variation (page 37) by 200% to bring to full size.

Stocking Heel

Enlarge template for the Christmas Stocking heel (page 34) by 133% to bring to full size.

Stocking Foot

Enlarge template tor the Christmas Stocking foot (page 34) by 133% to bring to full size.

Stocking Toe

Enlarge template for the Christmas Stocking toe (page 34) by 133% to bring to full size.

Stocking Cuff

Template for the Christmas Stocking cuff (page 34) shown at actual size.

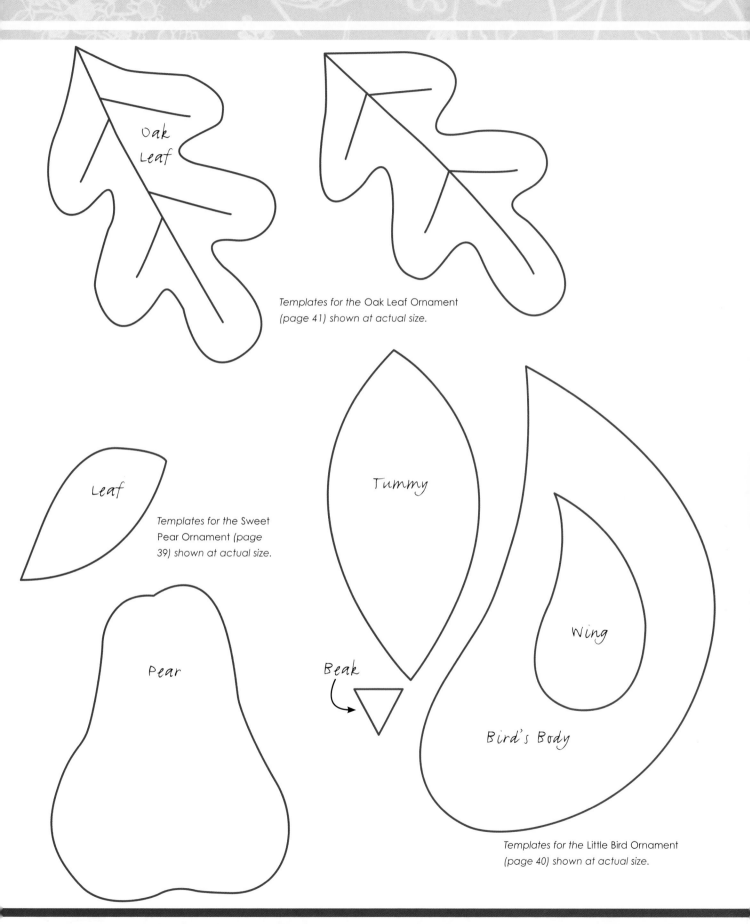

Oak
Leaf

Templates for the Oak Leaf Ornament (page 41) shown at actual size.

Leaf

Templates for the Sweet Pear Ornament (page 39) shown at actual size.

Pear

Tummy

Beak

Wing

Bird's Body

Templates for the Little Bird Ornament (page 40) shown at actual size.

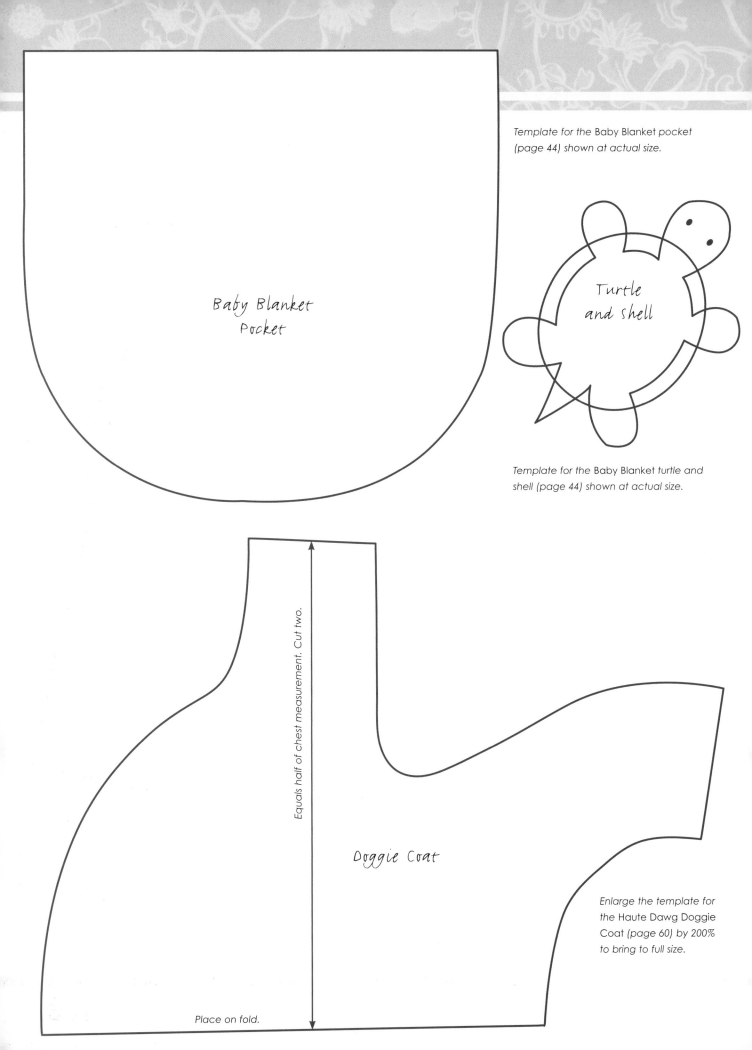

Baby Blanket
Pocket

Template for the Baby Blanket pocket
(page 44) shown at actual size.

Turtle
and shell

Template for the Baby Blanket turtle and
shell (page 44) shown at actual size.

Equals half of chest measurement. Cut two.

Doggie Coat

Enlarge the template for
the Haute Dawg Doggie
Coat (page 60) by 200%
to bring to full size.

Place on fold.

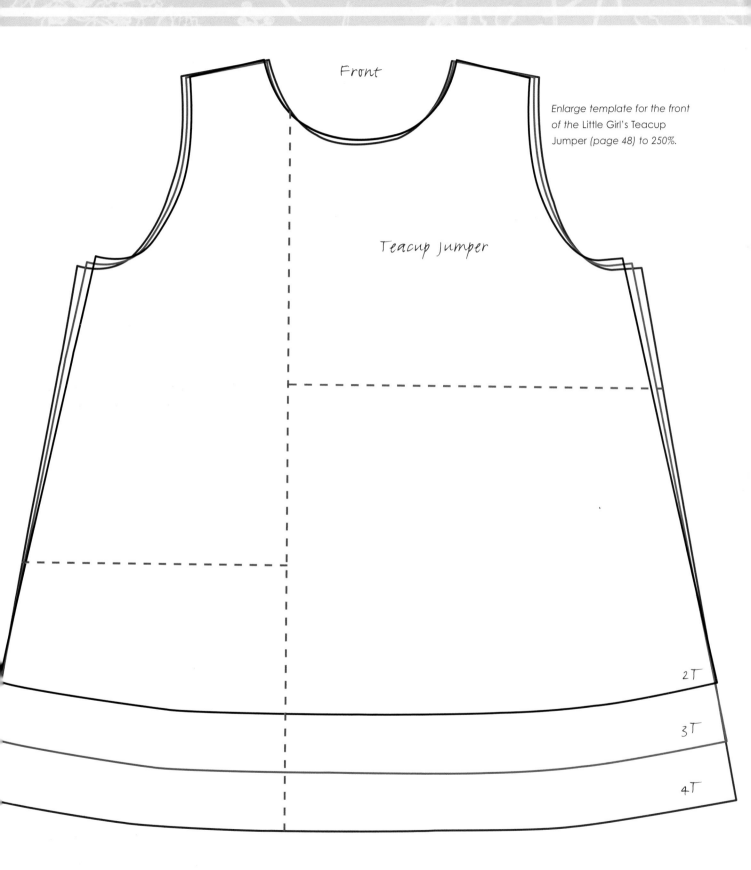

Front

Teacup Jumper

Enlarge template for the front of the Little Girl's Teacup Jumper (page 48) to 250%.

2T

3T

4T

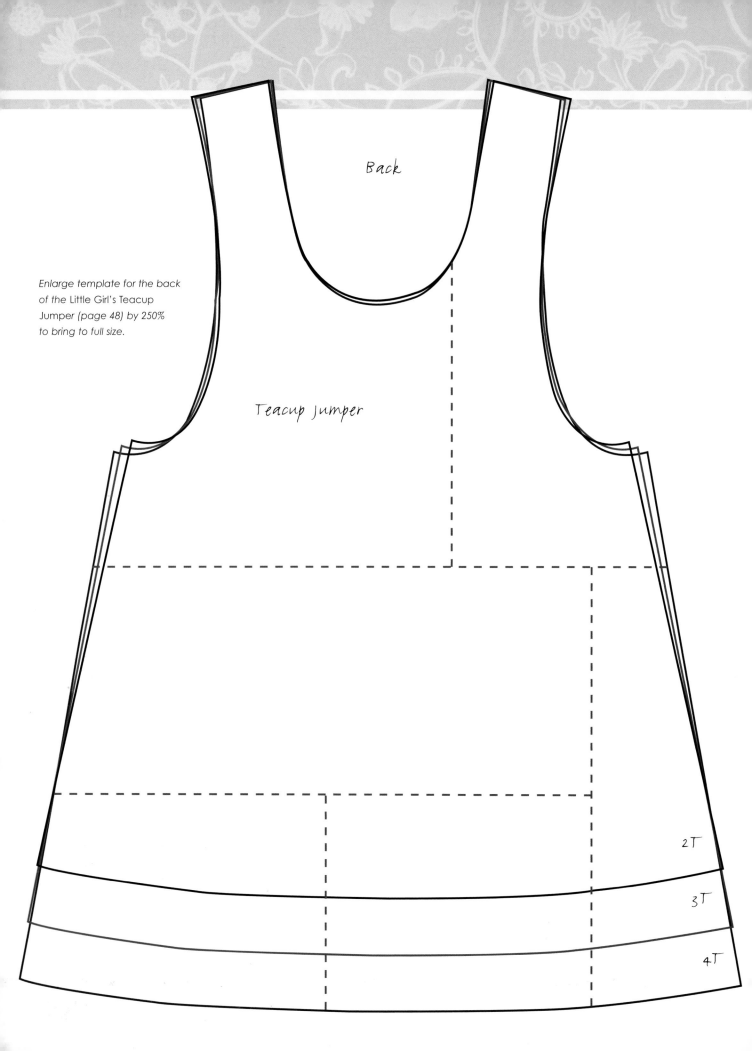

Back

Enlarge template for the back
of the Little Girl's Teacup
Jumper (page 48) by 250%
to bring to full size.

Teacup Jumper

2T

3T

4T

Overlap the pieces of the robot appliqué on
Boy's Robot Vest (page 52) as shown here.

Template for robot appliqué
on Boy's Robot Vest (page 52)
shown at actual size.

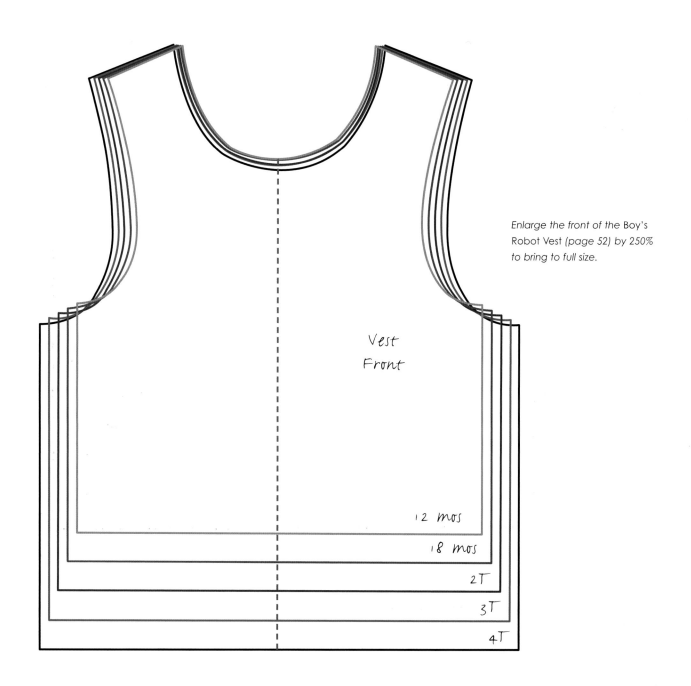

Vest
Front

Enlarge the front of the Boy's Robot Vest (page 52) by 250% to bring to full size.

12 mos
18 mos
2T
3T
4T

sizes	12 mos	18 mos	2T	3T	4T
Length from Shoulder	11½" (29cm)	12¼" (31cm)	13" (33cm)	13¾" (35cm)	14½" (37cm)
Chest	21" (53cm)	22" (56cm)	23" (58cm)	24" (61cm)	25" (64cm)

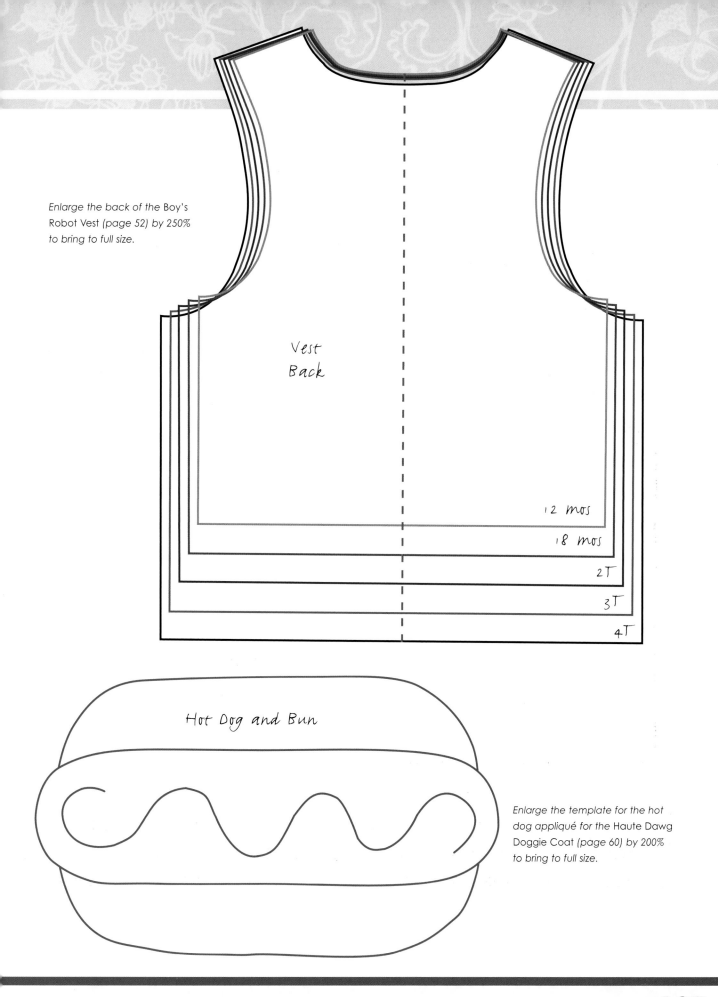

Enlarge the back of the Boy's Robot Vest (page 52) by 250% to bring to full size.

Vest Back

12 mos

18 mos

2T

3T

4T

Hot Dog and Bun

Enlarge the template for the hot dog appliqué for the Haute Dawg Doggie Coat (page 60) by 200% to bring to full size.

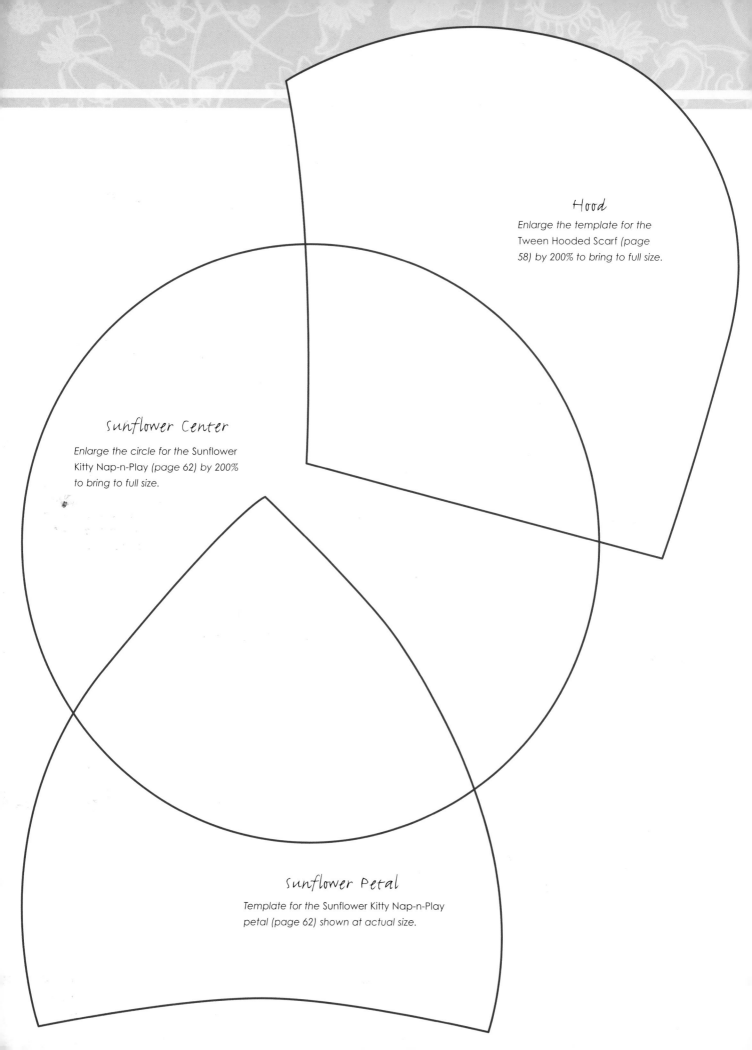

Hood

Enlarge the template for the Tween Hooded Scarf (page 58) by 200% to bring to full size.

Sunflower Center

Enlarge the circle for the Sunflower Kitty Nap-n-Play (page 62) by 200% to bring to full size.

Sunflower Petal

Template for the Sunflower Kitty Nap-n-Play petal (page 62) shown at actual size.

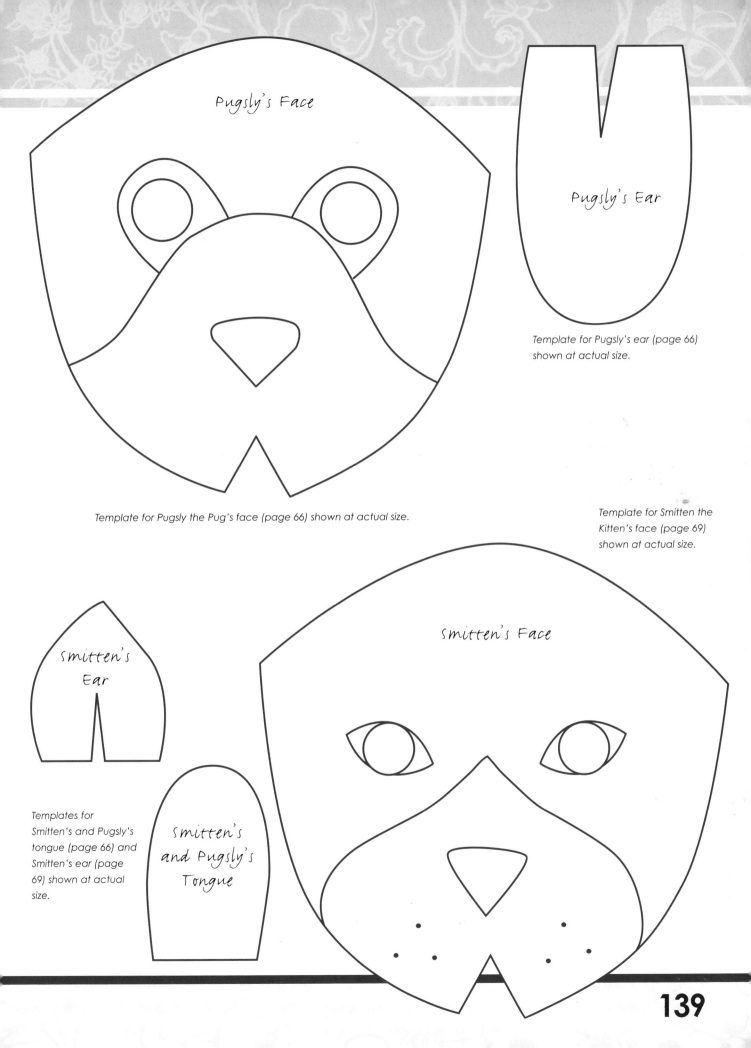

Pugsly's Face

Pugsly's Ear

Template for Pugsly's ear (page 66) shown at actual size.

Template for Pugsly the Pug's face (page 66) shown at actual size.

Template for Smitten the Kitten's face (page 69) shown at actual size.

Smitten's Face

Smitten's Ear

Smitten's and Pugsly's Tongue

Templates for Smitten's and Pugsly's tongue (page 66) and Smitten's ear (page 69) shown at actual size.

Top of Puppets' Mouths

Template for top of the Hand Puppets' mouths (both cat and dog, page 66) shown at actual size.

Bottom of Puppets' Mouths

Template for bottom of the Hand Puppets' mouths (both cat and dog, page 66) shown at actual size.

Puppets' Fronts

Template for bottom of the Hand Puppets (both cat and dog, page 66) shown at actual size.

Puppets' Backs

Template for back of the Hand Puppets (both cat and dog, page 66) shown at actual size.

Cone

Wrapper

Bonbon

Bonbon

Templates for the two
bonbons and their
wrapper in the Bonbon
Journal *(page 78)*
shown at actual size.

Ice Cream

Templates for the ice
cream and cone in the
Ice Cream Cone Tape
Measure *(page 76)*
shown at actual size.

Butterfly
Brooch

Sprouts Brooch
Leaf

Templates for the petal
and leaf of the Sprouts
Brooch *(page 105)* shown
at actual size.

Template for the
Butterfly Brooch
(page 107) shown
at actual size.

Sprouts Brooch
Petal

Template for the Pinwheel Brooch
(page 106) shown at actual size.

Template for the pin back for
Butterfly *(page 107)* shown at
actual size.

Butterfly
Pin Back

Pinwheel
Brooch

Pinwheel
Center

Template for pin back of
Sprouts *(page 105)* and
Pinwheel *(page 106)* shown
at actual size.

Sprouts &
Pinwheel
Pin Back

Template for center of
Pinwheel *(page 106)*
shown at actual size.

Bomber Hat Center Crown Panel
S/M–L/XL

Bomber Hat Earflap
S/M–L/XL

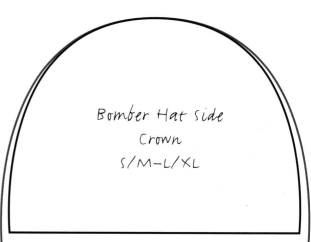

Bomber Hat Side
Crown
S/M–L/XL

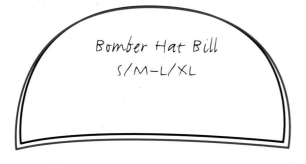

Bomber Hat Bill
S/M–L/XL

*Enlarge templates for the Bomber Hat
(page 122) by 250% to bring to full size.*

Index